The Afghanistan Papers

Part I

Interviews 1 - 10

Interview 1: Douglas Lute (Former White House war szar for Afghanistan)
Interview 2: Stephen Hadley (Former U.S. national security advisor)
Interview 3: Michael Flynn (Former U.s. Lietuenant general and national security adviser
Interview 4: Mari Strmecki (Former Rumsfeld advisor)
Interview 5: Robert Finn (Former U.S. ambassador to afghanistan)
Interview 6: Ryan Crocker (Retired U.S. diplomat)
Interview 7: Jeffrey Eggers (Former National Security Council staffer)
Interview 8: Brian Copes (Retired U.S. Army brigadier general)
Interview 9: Jefferey Eggers (Former National Security Council Staffer)
Interview 10: Richard Boucher (Retired U.S. Diplomat)

Lessons Learned Record of Interview

PROJECT NAME/ID
LL-01
Interview Title:
LL-01-d5
Interview with Ambassador Douglas Lute, NATO Permanent Rep, former Director Iraq/Afghanistan, NSC 2007-2014
Date/Time:
February 20, 2015; 07:45-08:45
Location:
US Mission to NATO, NATO HQ, Brussels, Belgium
Purpose:
To gain perspective on NSC strategy and planning processes on Afghanistan
SIGAR Attendees:
Candace Rondeaux, Krisanne Campos

Non- attribution Basis:	Yes		No	x	On the record
Recorded:	Yes		No	x	

Recording File Record Number:
n/a
Prepared By: (Name, title and date)
Krisanne Campos, Candace Rondeaux
Reviewed By: (Name, title and date)
n/a
Key Topics:
<ul><li>NSC organizational processes</li><li>Strategic assessment and review</li><li>Resource review for strategy</li></ul>

Lessons Learned Programs

An effective lessons learned program would be organic. If done from the outside it would generate antibodies, but nonetheless it's still a worthwhile effort.

NSC Organizational Processes

I did not have a lot of direct interaction with the NSC. My perspective from 2004-2007 is through CENTCOM and then the J3. The J3 typically does not attend NSC meetings. CENTCOM is invited on a

Lessons Learned Record of Interview

case-by-case basis. I would say until 2007, I had no direct interaction with the NSC. I had seen the "Convener" role of NSC from my seat on the Joint staff prior, but before my prominent role as "Director" I didn't have a view onto NSC processes. NSC took direction from DOD within Joint Staff.

From 2004-2007, during the Rumsfeld years, there was a tight leash on DOD. This coincides with my "outside" years. There was no huge role for the NSC at that point except for the PCs.

In 2006, big moves were made. There were the elections, Rumsfeld transitioned to Gates, and Petraeus took command in Iraq. In 2007, Hadley convinces the President that the NSC needs a bigger role. He needed a deputy to focus on Iraq and Afghanistan, whose attention would break down to about 85 percent on Iraq and 15 percent on Afghanistan, or maybe even 90 percent attention on Iraq and 10 percent attention on Afghanistan. This reflects the weight of effort regarding troop numbers. In 2007, Afghanistan was viewed as an "economy of force" – in other words, a secondary effort.

The scheme was to hire someone who knew the two conflicts and could relieve Hadley of the daily duties of advising the NSC. There was not much of a sense of strategy in the military sense – ways, means, and ends – but obviously there was a sense of policy; that's what the NSC does. However, there was not attention given to goals, methods, and resources, which is essentially what strategy is. The only professional group that does real strategy is the military. From that perspective, it's not hard to see where to contribute. Why should we have the expectation that outside the military the leadership knows how to do strategy? Hadley is a corporate lawyer; he is not schooled in policy. Susan Rice, Donilon – they are not schooled in this. Maybe they have some experience in policy, but definitely not strategy. Therefore, there is a heavy burden on the military for strategy development. It was not a rational process that determined the NSC needed a strategist; it felt like it happened randomly on a Tuesday. But there was a structural gap: there were two wars going on and we didn't have anyone speaking strategically. There was a gap, or a void, in trying to connect ends, ways, and means.

Resource Reviews and Strategy

The resource reviews come from a Clausewitzian strategic logic of ends, ways, and means. Strategy is the initial alignment of what you want to achieve – goals, or ends. The NSC is good at this part of policy; there is a healthy paragraph outlining goals in Afghanistan. The ends part is outlined by presidential directives, rhetoric, speeches. But below this, the trilogy or chain tends to get weaker.

As for ways, there is only a casual appreciation of how to deal with this part of the equation. There is an overemphasis on the military – an over-appreciation of the military and an under-appreciation of policy, diplomacy and development. These are all considered secondary to the primacy of military ways. This begins to fracture or erode strategy. We came to this realization late (i.e. Obama speech on hammer/nail).

Given *what* you're trying to achieve and *how* is where resources and resource reviews come in, but no one is tallying up the bill. If you over-rely on the military, there tends to be a fixation on troop numbers. It's as if the only dial in the engine room is troop numbers. Resource reviews discovered what other resources are in hand, and sometimes there are glaring findings. AID, for instance, was under-executing by more than half of its appropriations. There was a huge bubble in the pipeline and they couldn't catch up. The thought is that if we don't spend, GAO or committees on the Hill will stop us from getting more funding. This leads to spend, spend, spend. The reason this is happening: no one is paying attention in an interagency sense to resources.

Lessons Learned Record of Interview

The military, for instance, has over $1 billion in CERP money but does not at all coordinate with AID and no one can account for it – it was funny money! Classic case: you go to a PRT and they are almost completely reliant on CERP. There would be a State guy at the PRT totally out of his element saying, "No one pays any attention to me." There was a distorted view of development because of this overreliance on the military. Development objectives take on short-term time horizons to fit the military's short time horizons when development really needs long-term horizons.

Khost--Gardez road: There was criminal infiltration and the Taliban were making money on the fact that the road was never going to be completed. PRT commanders were flooding money into it, one-year money, to no result. Resource reviews showed us that if you only focused on the ends and ways, then there is no strategy; you are missing the means, or the resources. But they don't get down to strategy (where the money meets the road) because you don't have a strategy. The military gets this: tactical level – don't try to achieve something without the resources for it. Look at the bios for NSA advisors, except for Powell. You shouldn't expect them to come as strategic advisors because they don't have that sort of background. This shouldn't be a surprise.

I bumped into an even more fundamental lack of knowledge; we were devoid of a fundamental understanding of Afghanistan – we didn't know what we were doing. What are the demographics of the country? The economic drivers? AID: really? We're going to do something in Afghanistan with $10 billion? Haiti is a small country in our own backyard with no extremist insurgency and we can't develop it. And we expect to develop Afghanistan with $10 billion? Where we have the Pashtuns – a nation with no nation state with 60 percent living in Pakistan. What are we trying to do here? We didn't have the foggiest notion of what we were undertaking. We never would have tolerated rosy-goal statements if we understood, and this didn't really start happening until Obama. For example, the economy: we stated that our goal is to establish a "flourishing market economy." I thought we should have specified a flourishing drug trade – this is the only part of the market that's working. It's really much worse than you think. There is a fundamental gap of understanding on the front end, overstated objectives, an overreliance on the military, and a lack of understanding of the resources necessary.

DOD's budget is roughly $120 billion per year, which should include about $1 million per year per soldier. That means approximately $100 billion per year on soldiers alone. Did we really need the Burger Kings, gyms, bottled water shipped over the Arabian Sea? DOD's budget to build ANSF in 2010-2011 or 2011-2012 was the single largest item in the budget. It even exceeded the Joint Strike Fighter budget for two years. They were spending over $10 billion each year that was appropriated at $12 billion, and they realized they couldn't spend it all and had to give back $1 billion. We can't just shovel one-year money at this problem. You can't possibly build the ANSF that fast.

We were also pouring money into huge infrastructure projects to obligate money that was appropriated to show we could spend it. And we were building infrastructure in ways that Afghanistan could never sustain or even use in some cases.

One poignant example of this is a ribbon cutting ceremony complete with the giant scissors I attended for the district police chief in some God-forsaken province. It was a USACE-completed building with a glass façade and an atrium. The police chief couldn't even open the door; he had never seen a doorknob like this. To me, this encapsulates the whole experience in Afghanistan.

Lessons Learned Record of Interview

In terms of appropriations, Congress appropriated what the administration asked for. This had the distorting effect of having to support the troops. If you don't understand how ends, ways and means fit together (or maybe they don't even make sense in the first place), the simplest thing to do is to support the troops or support the Afghan troops so we can leave. I didn't see a lot of staff probing deeper. I mean, look who mans the staff committees: not strategists, but budgeters. We don't have a cross-government structure that is really focused on strategy.

Once in a while, ok, we can overspend. We are a rich country and can pour money down a hole and it doesn't bust the bank. But should we? Can't we get a bit more rational about this? Here's why not: because of the bureaucratic burdens between the different players. State, AID, and DOD are the big three and the sorts of organizational changes necessary to mandate that they are more rational on strategic questions of war won't be done from the bottom up – a lessons learned project won't break down barriers because these bureaucratic barriers are too strong.

DOD's own barriers were only broken down by Vietnam through Goldwater-Nichols. You need law to mandate reform, which in this case broke down the bureaucratic, stovepipe approach used in Vietnam. And this dealt only with the internal issues of one of the biggest players. We need a solution *across* the biggest players. With something like a "Goldwater-Nichols II" the problem would entail Congress reforming itself, particularly the Committee structures in Congress. If the American people knew the magnitude of this dysfunction…2,400 lives lost. Who will say this was in vain?

Keep in mind now that it's high political season here. The notion of being harshly introspective will be next to politically impossible. Maybe with a little more time and perspective it will not be as politicized. The military is the most culturally introspective organization. Still, they tend to do this at the lowest level, the tactical level, but don't do this as we move up the chain. Bolger's report was two-thirds about how the troops did tactically.

The 2014 withdrawal date was first announced in Karzai's inaugural speech in 2009. Spanta gave the speech to Karzai after Eikenberry added the statement that by the end of my [Karzai's] term, we [Afghans] should be fully responsible for our country (through ANSF), which translates to 2014.

At the NATO summit in Lisbon in 2010, a huge topic is Afghanistan, which is NATO's largest military operation. NATO takes note of Karzai's inauguration statement and write his statement into NATO's communiqué: Karzai couldn't refute it because he had in more or less words made the statement and this gave the coalition a horizon to aim for. To move a big coalition, you need two things: resources and a calendar. Obama has been setting strategic markers and end points on the calendar for achieving ends. This gave us a window to end or wrap up building ANSF. This was an opportunity to plant the flag, creating a closer horizon. Why not? Karzai had already said it. This focused DOD on the task at hand – building ANSF. There was an overemphasis on doing the military effort ourselves; we were predominantly doing it ourselves and discounting Afghan capacity and means. There was an under resourced advisory effort (for the ANSF) for years. So this planted the flag and forced DOD to build the ANSF as a priority. I'd say it worked, mostly.

The NATO Lisbon communiqué stated that beyond 2014, NATO accepts and Afghanistan welcomes continuing efforts at 1/10 the current size, which is now Resolute Support. In Chicago, we arrived at another benchmark – a date to transition to a non-combat mission.

The problem is that in the meantime, we had surged. A fundamental impact of the surge was to westernize the fight – we committed to do it ourselves, not through Afghans. So who was doing the advisory effort? We economized. We got the ANSF we deserve. If we started with ANSF in 2002-

Lessons Learned Record of Interview

2006 when the Taliban was weak and disorganized, things may have been different. Instead, we went to Iraq. If we committed money deliberately and sooner, we could have a different outcome.

LESSONS LEARNED RECORD OF INTERVIEW

Project Title and Code:	
Strategy and Planning – LL-01	
Interview Title:	
Interview with former National Security Advisor Stephen Hadley	
Interview Code:	
LL-01-d12	
Date/Time:	
September 16, 2015 / 14:40-15:20	
Location:	
United States Institute of Peace, Headquarters, Washington, D.C.	
Purpose:	
To solicit Mr. Hadley's views on strategy development and implementation within the National Security Council and the interagency during the early years of the post-2001 intervention.	
Interviewees: (Either list interviewees below, attach sign-in sheet to this document or hyperlink to a file)	
Mr. Stephen Hadley	
SIGAR Attendees:	
Scott Worden, Matthew Sternenberger, and LL-01 Project Lead	
Sourcing Conditions (On the Record/On Background/etc.): **On the Record**	
Recorded: Yes ☐ No ☒	
Recording File Record Number (if recorded): N/A	
Prepared By: (Name, title and date)	
Matthew Sternenberger, Research Analyst, 9/21/2015	
Reviewed By: (Name, title and date)	
Key Topics:	
• Initial Thoughts on the U.S. Strategy in Afghanistan • Accelerating Success Initiative • Post-Conflict Planning • Warlord Strategy • Multilateralism • National Security Council	

Interview at USIP HQ with Stephen Hadley former National Security Advisor to President George W. Bush from 2005 to 2009. Additionally, Mr. Hadley served as Deputy National Security Advisor from 2001 to 2005, as a principal at the Scowcroft Group from 1993 to 2001, and as Assistant Secretary of Defense for International Security Policy from 1989-1993.

Initial Thoughts on the U.S. Strategy in Afghanistan

1. Our strategy was a declaration against international terrorism. There was a strategy but it looks different when you compare it to Iraq, where we had time to plan. When 9/11 happened we had to plan on the fly.

LESSONS LEARNED RECORD OF INTERVIEW

2. The strategy for Afghanistan was embedded in the Global War on Terror (GWOT) and we can't hive off Iraq or Afghanistan as both were central to the GWOT. The goal was to take the fight to the enemy abroad so we did not have to fight them at home. There was a kinetic phase and then an ideological phase based on using the idea of freedom and democracy as an alternative vision to terrorism and to counter the appeal of al Qaeda.
3. It was also about hardening the homeland.
4. The White House was also focused on preventing the return of al Qaeda to Afghanistan. In light of the 1980s and the U.S. support for the mujahedeen against the Soviets. We released the furies and then went home. This piece required us to build a resilient Afghanistan for the people and do so in a democratic framework to strengthen the government so that they [the Afghan government] could resist al Qaeda so we don't have to come back. We originally said that we won't do nation building but there is no way to ensure that al Qaeda won't come back without it.

What we did not want to do was avoid the lessons from previous eras. We know Afghanistan has an allergy to outsiders and the presence of the outsiders stimulate potent antibodies. If we do go in, we can't go in as conquerors, but rather as enablers. The Taliban was overthrown by less than 1,000 Special Forces and CIA personnel, but they were largely in an enabling role. This [enabling role] made this different from the Soviets and British times. We were not seen as occupiers and most Afghans wanted the U.S. to stay which vindicated us.

The different components of the interagency did not want to become occupiers or to overwhelm the Afghans. But once the Taliban was flushed, we didn't want to throw that progress away. We were reluctant to ramp up a large number of forces in fear that we would be seen as occupiers. The reconstruction piece was an element meant to better peoples' lives. **The challenge was doing reconstruction in the fifth poorest country in the world that had little absorptive capacity and human capital. We needed to be careful about how to meter in assistance money without it leading to corruption or inflation – both which are destabilizing to the economy. As we did start to pump in money during the late Bush years and early Obama years, we ended up with both inflation and corruption.**

Accelerating Success Initiative (ASI)

The main person you [SIGAR] will want to talk to is Zal [Khalilzad]. Accelerating Success Initiative did not involve all that much money, about $1.5 billion or so and meant to empower and enable Afghanistan. It was also about building infrastructure. This was the one time we did it right. Robin Cleveland set up a separate OMB process that went in parallel with the program creation process. We had a program and an integrated funding piece. *The OMB did their financial process in concert with the policy planning at the NSC. It was a great idea, but I don't think we have done something like that again.*

Post-Conflict Planning

In Iraq, contrary to Afghanistan, we had the chance to do post-war planning. **Franklin Miller** is the one to talk to about this. He got the Deputies Committee involved. At one point I was visited by [General] Jim McCarthy, who I believe is now with Johns Hopkins. He was asked by the Defense Science Board to see what happened with all the post-war and post-conflict planning efforts. He found that they existed but there was no process within the Office of Secretary of Defense or the Joint Chiefs to transfer planning into operational guidance that would reach down to the platoon level. [See report here.] In the military, however, they can take things like the campaign plans down to the foot soldier. Everyone knows their role and what to do. There was just no process to do post-war mission planning or how to give guidance. This structural problem still exists. When I was abroad I would run into Captains who had no idea what they were supposed to be doing. *If you create planning documents they need to be operationalized into guidance in the field – the Department of Defense (DOD) just didn't have that. It was astonishing.*

LESSONS LEARNED RECORD OF INTERVIEW

Warlord Strategy

Well Zal [Khalilzad] is the man for this. He was the one doing it and felt strongly that we needed to sideline the warlords. There were two main strategies to implement it. There was a questions as to whether to do it top down or bottom up. First, it was top-down and involved us negotiating with the warlords. It meant bringing them into Kabul and giving them a fancy title. The second was to take away their troops to get them out. No troops meant no power. In the end, we did a combination of both: [Disarmament, Demobilizations & Reintegration] DDR with Japanese funding and lured them to Kabul.

My impression was that it [the warlord strategy] largely worked at first. The threats from warlords decreased dramatically from 2003 to 2005. During this same period, however, the Taliban threat was increasing. We were taking people out of the fight just as the Talibs were getting back to the fight. I asked Zal, 'Are you sure about this? We're taking people out of the game when we needed them to fight.' Zal said that the country [Afghanistan] remembers the Soviet coup, the civil war period and warlord rule. They did not want to return to warlord rule. Most [warlords] undermined the authorities and other efforts to build an Afghan army. After 2005, my impression was that the warlords were back because Karzai wanted them back and he only understood the patronage system. Karzai was never sold on democracy and did not rely on democratic institutions, but instead relied on patronage. Because of his reliance on patronage, they [warlords] made a comeback.

Multilateralism

As with all reconstruction efforts, the goal was to help Afghanistan build a government, provide a prosperous life for the Afghan people, and thus create a resiliency against al Qaeda's return. The question became how to organize it. We were bashed for being unilateral but I don't know how bringing in 28 nations into a coalition is unilateral. We brought in others by building the International Security Assistance Force and divvying up the country. The next questions was how to do the security piece of state building. Under the multilateral approach we again divided up the different sectors such as police training and justice sector reform. **With this [multilateral] approach, everyone had small pieces of the sector and it then meant that it became everyone's second or third order priority so nothing got done.** In Iraq we did this same job with a U.S. and DOD lead. We still have never solved the police training problem. **We just don't have a post-conflict stabilization model that works. Every time we have one of these things, it is a pick-up game. I don't have confidence that if we did it again, we would do any better.**

National Security Council (NSC)

The interagency process that we have today was designed by [Henry] Kissinger and Zbigniew Brzesinski. So it's 40 years old. The NSC is meant to develop policy options for the president and to get his decision. Developing an implementation strategy with Afghanistan was difficult because of the civ-mil integration problem and all the other aspects of post-conflict stabilization; we just didn't have a process to manage implementation. The NSC system was designed to get decisions by the president sent to various agencies to actually implement it but we had no way of pushing decisions downward. There's no mechanism for monitoring the implementation. The Afghan Operations Group (AOG aka AIOG) was an attempt to focus the NSC on implementation. The Deputies Committee is supposed to go forward to coordinate effective ways of implementing it and to ensure it got done with a sense of urgency. We would get all the agencies that had pieces to implement together and sit at a table twice a week. They would take the decisions from the Deputies Committee meeting and put them into an implementation plan. We would break up responsibilities and then track them with the traffic light charts. This was a precursor to what we had Lute do. **The Tower Commission Report said that the NSC has a role in implementing and execution. I believe that the NSC should not do implementation but that it does have the responsibility to see that it policy implementation did get done with urgency.**

Record of Meeting with Stephen Hadley 09/16/15

UNITED STATES OF AMERICA

+ + + + +

SPECIAL INSPECTOR GENERAL

FOR AFGHANISTAN RECONSTRUCTION

+ + + + +

INTERVIEW OF: AMBASSADOR RYAN CROCKER

Thursday, January 11, 2016

BEFORE:
DR. CANDACE RONDEAUX
JAMES WASSERSTROM
KATE BATEMAN

This transcript was produced from audio provided by the Special Inspector General for Afghanistan Reconstruction.

P-R-O-C-E-E-D-I-N-G-S

{time not provided}

AMBASSADOR CROCKER: -- (proceedings in progress) from different what SIGAR did in Iraq, hard lessons.

DR. RONDEAUX: So, it's different in the sense that this is -- though it's a substantial report, you know, fairly long, it's not a book.

In fact, the idea was really to stay away from doing a sort of 300 novelistic treatment of the entire epic of all things Afghanistan, because it's just too hard to read, too hard to distribute and doesn't really reach our primary audience in a way that makes sense, and our primary audience is Congress, as far as we're concerned, and then, you know, the secondary leader being the Executive Branch. So, that's one way in which it's very different.

I think the second way in which it's very different is that the program is led primarily by subject matter experts, like myself, like Jim, like Kate as well as others, who have spent time in Afghanistan, either beyond the wire, as I did, as an analyst and journalist or you know, inside the wire working on coordinating the policy and executing it.

So, that's a very substantial difference, in the sense that I think, you know, SIGAR was more about -- led by generalists, who had kind of a broad understanding, but couldn't get down into the weeds.

Lastly, I'd say, you know, the substantial difference is, you know, we have a time continuum where we're trying to get out a number of reports here, and we also envision the use of quantitative data to help back us up a little bit better.

We've dug very deep on, you know, an analysis of the cycles of obligation and disbursement, and how that sort of led to gaps in the disbursement of resources and programming, and what that meant, you know, for the political impact of the overall policies and programs and strategies in Afghanistan.

So, I think those are the three substantial differences.

AMBASSADOR CROCKER: Yes, that's pretty clear. Yes, I was much involved in hard lessons, but that was a -- a Washington centric effort, in how it was put together. As a field guy, I would incline myself more to what you're doing.

MR. WASSERSTROM: This is Jim Wasserstrom, Ambassador. I served with you, under you in the Embassy. I was there from 2010 to 2014.

So, I was the senior advisor of anti-corruption with the interagency law office.

AMBASSADOR CROCKER: Right.

MR. WASSERSTROM: The purpose behind my project is really to look at the evolution and the US reception and response to corruption over the period in question, 2001 to 2014, and using empathetic reconstruction to get a sense of how the US government initially perceived the problem, whether it did, and what were the manifestations of that perception and then, over time, how that perception evolved and what were the responses to the problem, not looking at corruption in Afghanistan per se, because of course, we could write thousands of pages on that, but really looking at what was the US role in the problem, but the perception and response, and what we did -- what we might have done better and differently looking in hindsight.

So, the lessons learned aspect of this is looking at the various -- at how corruption impinged on the agenda, and what priority was given to it, what were the intervening factors that may have shifted that priority, what superceded it?

Was there a conflict between corruption and other objectives, such as counter-terrorism among others, and then with the benefit of hindsight and wisdom, what might we have done better and differently with what we know now, and when would we have done that, and what with the -- what we might specifically advise for future interventions, because of course, the purposes of a lessons learned program is not necessarily, you know, to -- not only to analyze the past, but also to come up with generalizable lessons that we can apply to what's being planned now current, and for future interventions.

So, those are the two purposes behind our call today.

AMBASSADOR CROCKER: Okay.

DR. RONDEAUX: So, if we could start actually, just to give you a sense, we have done, at least for our project, probably I'd say 120 interviews so far, maybe more actually, at this stage, and what we're trying to do, if we can, is to work with particularly senior level officials like yourself, to make sure that the conversation is on the record, wherever and whenever possible, so that one, there's no sort of controversies, but two, more importantly, I just think for the sake of accuracy, fairness and balance, if we can do that, that would be preferred.

However, recognizing that sometimes that things that you want to say can be sensitive. If you want to go on background, we would appreciate it if you could tell us that in advance. If you want to go off the record, please let us know that, as well. Does that work for you?

AMBASSADOR CROCKER: Yes, there's not much point in doing this, if it's not on the record.

DR. RONDEAUX: Excellent. So, maybe I should start just with some generalized questions.

I mean, you were there in the early days, and we just spoke with your colleague Ambassador DAUBINS {phonetic} a few hours ago, and you know, he had a very interesting take on things.

I think -- I would imagine you share that, which is that, you know, at the outset, it seemed like the US government really wasn't -- you know, obviously caught by surprise by the attacks, but it was really positioned in the sense of having a baseline assessment of what was actually happening in Afghanistan vis-a-vis the economy, vis-a-vis security.

What's your estimation, when you walked into the picture early on, of what we actually knew about the state of affairs, both politically and economically and security-wise in Afghanistan?

AMBASSADOR CROCKER: Well, I was parachuted in, if you will. I was not a South Asian specialist, by any means. I was just asked to go out and get the Embassy open.

So, I had no real background in Afghanistan, past or present, and since I moved out on 72 hours notice, had no time to acquire anything.

So, to me, the whole emphasis was on just getting a mission up and running, which was no small challenge under the circumstances, and then kind of dealing with the -- the issues of the present.

I did have some people out there, like MATRINCO {phonetic}, Alan Err, who did have some background and were quite helpful to me in that regard.

But you know, just given the highly operational nature of my mission, I was not -- not really focused on how much we knew beforehand and how it related to what we were uncovering on the ground. It was all about what we were uncovering on the ground.

DR. RONDEAUX: What did you find when you arrived?

AMBASSADOR CROCKER: Absolute devastation. It seemed to me that coming into the city, primarily for the first time, I used the image often, reminded me of pictures of Berlin in 1945, and Kabul airport was closed at the time. You had to come in from Bagram, and driving through mile after mile of basically lifeless lug, having to forge, you know, a river because the bridge was out.

It was a very sobering experience, that there was almost literally nothing there, and that of course, was reinforced by my early meetings with KARZI {phonetic} who arrived only a couple of weeks before I did, that here was a leader of interim authority, who had no real authority and nothing to work with, no military, no police, no civil service, no functioning society.

So, the enormity of the task kind of hit me significantly right at the outset.

DR. RONDEAUX: It was a big task. It would have required -- certainly, it seems to me, everybody understood it was going to take years, but even opening the Embassy, you know, we talked with Ambassador Finn, as well.

I mean, he describes kind of the living conditions for folks early on and the challenges there.

I mean, to you when you arrived, what was the first priority, in terms of getting things up and running?

AMBASSADOR CROCKER: Well, as always in anything remotely comparable to that, in that part of the world, the first thing was security.

We had a company of Marines actually on the Embassy compound. So, I spent my first day walking the perimeter with the Marine company commander and the RSO, going through preparations, just being as sure as I could be, that we had a position, a facility that could be adequately defended if it had to be, and if you haven't got security, you haven't got anything.

Then after that, it was starting to build an on the ground relationship with the interim authority and KARZI in particular.

You made a comment earlier about it was going to be an enormous task that would take years. Well, at that point, we didn't know what the task was, you know, what the US was there to do, and as you know, there was -- in those early months, significant differences in view, in Washington, as to whether we should embark on a long term nation building effort or whether we wanted to keep our role and our agenda very minimal.

So, again, during the early-going path to reconstruction of Afghanistan with the -- an enormous multi-year task, obviously no question, but not clear that we would be the ones leading that effort.

DR. RONDEAUX: Not clearly because of that politic, but also I guess it was probably difficult to define.

I mean, you said security was the first concern, certainly for the Embassy. But it also seemed to be such a huge driving force in how we define the central pillar of all things strategic.

interim authority and KARZI in particular.

You made a comment earlier about it was going to be an enormous task that would take years. Well, at that point, we didn't know what the task was, you know, what the US was there to do, and as you know, there was -- in those early months, significant differences in view, in Washington, as to whether we should embark on a long term nation building effort or whether we wanted to keep our role and our agenda very minimal.

So, again, during the early-going path to reconstruction of Afghanistan with the -- an enormous multi-year task, obviously no question, but not clear that we would be the ones leading that effort.

DR. RONDEAUX: Not clearly because of that politic, but also I guess it was probably difficult to define.

I mean, you said security was the first concern, certainly for the Embassy. But it also seemed to be such a huge driving force in how we define the central pillar of all things strategic.

everybody understood it was going to take years, but even opening the Embassy, you know, we talked with Ambassador Finn, as well.

I mean, he describes kind of the living conditions for folks early on and the challenges there.

I mean, to you when you arrived, what was the first priority, in terms of getting things up and running?

AMBASSADOR CROCKER: Well, as always in anything remotely comparable to that, in that part of the world, the first thing was security.

We had a company of Marines actually on the Embassy compound. So, I spent my first day walking the perimeter with the Marine company commander and the RSO, going through preparations, just being as sure as I could be, that we had a position, a facility that could be adequately defended if it had to be, and if you haven't got security, you haven't got anything.

Then after that, it was starting to build an on the ground relationship with the

There is some debate about, you know, our levels of investment early on, but given that ambiguity, it seems to me that it was only natural, in some ways, that the lead nation approach kind of came to the floor. Can you talk about sort of what you saw, in terms of the -- how that emerged?

AMBASSADOR CROCKER: Well, as you know, again, I think reflecting to a certain tenure in Washington, that we did not want this to be an entirely American project.

There was an effort from the outset, to involve others, to involve NATO nations, in particular, and I saw that, you know, within the 30 days I was there, I think, where you know, we would have the primary responsibility for security, the Brits would counter-narcotics, the Italians would do police. I can't remember who else had what.

But you know, that multi-lateral approach to reconstruction was certainly an element right from the beginning.

DR. RONDEAUX: Looking back on that, do

you feel like there might have been a better path? I mean, I know we had no choice in some ways, but many people point to the lead nation approach as kind of one of those points on the map, where things began to kind of get out of kilter.

AMBASSADOR CROCKER: Well, that's why I look forward to reading what you write, because now, the (inaudible) had problems, no question.

Whether there was a better approach, I find that a little hard to answer because the only other two alternatives that I would see would be either a decision that there simply would not be a comprehensive reconstruction effort, which would have been pretty hard to justify and defend, given the extraordinary conditions in the country, and the suffering of the Afghan people.

The other option, of course, would be to say that the United States is going to lead and it's going to lead across the board.

You know, given the investment and blood and treasure that had transpired anyway, not within my capacity to say an American lead across the board would have been a good approach, but to me, it just seems that there are those three possibilities, a multi-lateral approach, a decision not to have a comprehensive redevelopment effort or a US-lead effort.

DR. RONDEAUX: Yes, I think -- I mean, that's right. I don't think we make any conclusions in our own -- at least my analysis about that, except to say that it was clear that, you know, certainly in the NSC, there was a great concern that having an American lead would just replicate the Soviet experience, and that this was, you know --

AMBASSADOR CROCKER: Sorry, which experience?

DR. RONDEAUX: The Soviet experience.

AMBASSADOR CROCKER: Soviet experience, right.

DR. RONDEAUX: Right, so having yet another sort of imperial power, as it were, come into the region and replay the dramas of the past was certainly many people's minds in the early days of the planning process.

AMBASSADOR CROCKER: Yes, I remember, you know, when this was determined, feeling a sense of some relief, at least I wasn't going to have to worry about everything.

You know, I remember a meeting with the Italians and the Brit, for example, and coming out of those meetings just glad that somebody else had to worry about whatever it was, policing.

DR. RONDEAUX: But it did come with challenges, in terms of coordination. Could you talk about the challenges of coordinating with five or six different lead nations, what you saw?

AMBASSADOR CROCKER: I wasn't there long enough to -- to really see that, because again, I was only out there for three months or so, and with the -- was pretty well caught up in just trying to make our own efforts work.

You know, in that period, first week in March 2002, that we launched Operation Anaconda, which did not go well for us, and caused us to kind of reconsider what our -- you know, our own posture needed to be, in terms of security, I was spending a whole lot of time working with the -- the CIA and the military on force structures and roles and missions and so forth.

So, you know, coordination on other elements of reconstruction was not just something I really got much into in those first weeks.

You've talked to Robert Finn so --

DR. RONDEAUX: Yes.

AMBASSADOR CROCKER: Yes.

DR. RONDEAUX: Yes, we definitely have a better sense of that.

AMBASSADOR CROCKER: Yes, and --

DR. RONDEAUX: Yes, we have. So, maybe we should fast-forward. I don't want to skip too many years, obviously.

But you know, you come in much -- into the picture much later and find a different Afghanistan.

AMBASSADOR CROCKER: Yes, and the Afghanistan I found, for me, and throughout my time there, the second time, was very much a glass half full or more than half full.

It's all relative, because my frame of reference was the absolute devastation of early 2002, and what I came back to was -- for all of the problems, was light years beyond that.

DR. RONDEAUX: What do you think were the contributing factors to that shift?

AMBASSADOR CROCKER: You know, after, again, you know this painfully well, after years of an economy of force operation, when we finally did ramp up militarily, you know, it clearly had an impact on the overall security situation, and by the time I came back, it allowed some significant steps to be taken in areas such as health and education.

Infrastructure, my focus in the early going had been to get a commitment from the US to develop physical infrastructure, focused mainly on roads, and of course, by the time I came back, the ring road had been completely reconstructed and you know, the difference that made, in terms again, primarily of security, but also just in the -- of the -- the ability of people to access schools, access healthcare, to move goods around, you know, just a marked difference.

I had an early focus on education, as you know, we got an education program launched almost immediately after the fall of the Taliban. There was no female education whatsoever.

We had a girls school opened in January of 2002, and I remember going to visit that, and you know, it was kids basically sitting on the floor, using mimeographed materials, and this is a first grade class and the girls were everywhere from six to 12, because the 12 year olds, of course, had been of primary school age when the Taliban came though, and you know, just again, thinking how little there was, how much deprivation there was and how hard all this would be to improve on.

So, coming back, I can't remember what the stats were when I got there in 2011, but you know, the number of kids in school, the number of girls in school was more than I would have even hoped for, when we were just getting started.

DR. RONDEAUX: There was also another phenomenon that was kind of obsessively talked about at that time.

I mean, you know, for Afghan's, I think this phenomenon was an ever-present part of their life, whether or not it was always something that resinated with their American counterparts, and that -- that was the problem of corruption.

I want to open the floor to my colleagues to talk about that, but I am just curious about sort of, your general impressions when you returned in 2011, of that phenomenon, how it impacted your ability to do your job.

AMBASSADOR CROCKER: Yes, again, corruption was not something I spent any time on, the first time around, and that would be -- if you will, a negative difference coming back, because you know, no question about the scale of corruption.

In one of my initial conversations with (inaudible), you know, we had (inaudible). Again, all of the mechanisms that you know so well.

But I was struck by something KARZI said and repeated a number of times during my tenure, which is that the west led by the US, in his clear view, had a significant responsibility to bear for the whole corruption issue.

You know, I know what oath the military and USAID said about all the steps that were being taken to ensure that contracts were not subject to corruption, but I -- I always thought KARZI had a point, that you just cannot put those amounts of money into a very fragile state and society, and not have it fuel corruption. You just can't.

As we look at how we might ever do this again, that to me, is a really big issue, because you know, we've got the same thing in Iraq, where corruption is now some pandemic and deeply rooted, it's hard to see how a better political order and ever be established, that one thing the -- the have's, if you will, agree on, I think in both countries, however they may be divided on other political issues is, they like the current system because it pays.

So, having been through this now twice, Iraq and Afghanistan, one of the profound questions I would ask, if we ever, God forbid, look at something on such a scale again, is how do you do it in a way that does not inadvertently fuel wholesale corruption?

MS. BATEMAN: Sir, do you have any concrete thoughts on an answer to that questions?

MR. WASSERSTROM: We're all ears, I have to tell you.

AMBASSADOR CROCKER: Yes, well, I think the first thing -- I mean, one thing I would say is that you need to have the corruption framing everything you propose to do, in terms of development and reconstruction, and to overcome the instinctive American urge to do a whole lot and to do it tomorrow, to understand that if you try to do that, not only are there fundamental capacity questions and everything else you've been dealing with over the years, but that you will inevitably be fueling large scale corruption.

So, to throttle it back, so you're

operating at a level where you can monitor, even if that is less than we American's would like to do it, it certainly will be, but you know, given what's happened again, in Iraq, as well as Afghanistan, you know, we've got to have the corruption lense in place, right at the outset of, not just development and reconstruction efforts, but the whole formulation of a reconstruction strategy.

MR. WASSERSTROM: Can I ask you -- this is Jim Wasserstrom, again, Ambassador.

You're referring specifically to reconstruction and so on, but one of the recurring themes that we -- that we hear, is also with the military's substantial footprint, as it grew over time, having fueled corruption through its demands for logistics and fuel and so on.

Would you agree with that, the sense of that statement?

AMBASSADOR CROCKER: Well, broadly speaking, I mean, yes. You know, again, you've got a very significant military presence. It requires a whole lot of stuff for maintenance and substance and in a sense, our military, you know, no longer kind of maintains an inherent capacity to do those things, because it's just too expensive, it takes too many people. It's going to be out-sourced.

When you're out-sourcing on that scale, in that weak of a society, with the time pressures that go along with it, you know, then you get the corruption.

I think it's a great point that you're making, because it's not -- I was focused really on developmental issues, but you know, the amount of money that went into military contracts, probably more towards even that.

So, what you may be looking at, in the amount and way of modern War, it is a virtual guarantee of corruption.

You know, our military cannot support itself, but itself, and I don't see any way we're ever going to reverse that because of the expenses, and that means we're getting goods and services from others, and you know, the time imperative and the scale make it very hard for me to see how you can ever do that, without fueling corruption at the same time.

I mean, it's -- it's worth a lot of your time, I think to kind of look at that question, can we fight -- or can we maintain a substantial momentary presence in conflict conditions, without inadvertently fueling corruption?

MR. WASSERSTROM: Yes, yes. Critical tradeoff, certainly.

I'd like to turn maybe to a case study of all of this, which is the delightful story of the collapse of Kabul Bank.

AMBASSADOR CROCKER: Yes.

MR. WASSERSTROM: I'm sure something with which you are well familiar and I was there during that period too, and how painful it all was.

How did that -- how did -- for you as the Ambassador during a critical period, how did you approach that issue? What were the -- there were obviously cross-currents that existed. We had many different priorities.

The Kabul Bank was such a huge issue for quite a long period of time, the theft of one-billion dollars. So, what were the -- what was your thinking as you addressed the issue, both with Washington and with KARZI?

AMBASSADOR CROCKER: Well, the Kabul Bank, of course, it happened before I got there.

MR. WASSERSTROM: Yes.

AMBASSADOR CROCKER: So, for me, it was -- you know, there was not the immediate crisis. It was how do you -- how do you deal with this in a way that would give both donor nations and Afghan's themselves, the sense that not only, what controls would you put in place to prevent something like that ever happening again, but that there would be accountability.

I have lost track of the number of conversations I had with KARZI and any number of others, about the accountability issue, and you know, promises were made, some steps were taken, but I've seen the recent reporting, you know, on Kabul Bank, and all that -- really, there never was an accounting.

You know, by the time I had left, it was fairly clear to me that again, given the entrenched nature of corruption and the extent to which the establishment, you know, including KARZI's own family, as well as (inaudible), that it was highly unlikely that steps would be taken to bring people to account.

You know, I had conversations with ASHRA FATI {phonetic} who would rail about this, and I think we all thought when he came into office, that maybe finally something would happen.

But I think what we're seeing clearly is what I was talking about earlier, that the deep rooted nature of corruption, whether it's Kabul Bank or anything else, is now beyond the ability of even a determined Afghan President to correct.

I used to go over to SOLIS's {phonetic} house to talk about these things, because he felt that the chances were pretty good that his house wasn't bugged, unlike his office, and you know, he -- you know, effectively said, it's bad, it's really bad and I can't do anything about it.

MR. WASSERSTROM: Yes.

DR. RONDEAUX: You know, the good thing about {phonetic} KHAN is that he is dead.

AMBASSADOR CROCKER: Yes, and I check just about every other day, and as far as I know, he is still dead.

DR. RONDEAUX: You know, and as an old journalist hand, you know, you can't liable the dead. So, I'm wondering if we can talk about him a little bit more, and kind of his role, because he was around actually -- his role was really peaking.

What was your understanding of how much control he had, for instance, over the military, and this would have -- the sort of corruption, particularly with regard to the use of fuel resources and air assets?

AMBASSADOR CROCKER: Yes, I met KHAN my first time out, and amid a lot of colorful personalities, he made a particular impression on me.

One graphic moment, it was the time of the HODGE {phonetic} and not surprisingly, the early 2002, the charters got all messed up. You had people stranded at the airports and in bitterly cold temperatures for hours, if not days. It was the Minister of civil aviation that was suppose to be in charge of that.

One night, John McCall, the British force commander and I were meeting with KARZI fairly and (Inaudible) KHAN walked into the room. He was giggling, and he proceeded to relate to us that a mob had gotten out of control at the airport and had murdered the Minister of civil aviation, and he giggled while he related this.

Later, much later, it emerged, I don't know if it was every verified or not, it emerged that KHAN himself had the Minister killed.

But I certainly came out of those opening months with the feeling that even by Afghan standards, I was in the presence of a totally evil person.

When I came back, my sense of him was

that he was not directly involved in major strategy or operational decisions, that he was more interested in making even more elicit millions, but that KARZI had to handle him with real care, because he could be dangerous and no question in my mind, he could be dangerous.

But my impression of him the second time around is that relatively speaking, he was less of a factor than he was the first time around, to which I gave considerable (inaudible).

DR. RONDEAUX: That's interesting, actually, so, I'm intrigued. I spent a lot of time looking at KHAN and his friends, and I'm just sort of intrigued by a couple of things, I guess.

If you remember, the National Military Hospital scandal, that also kind of unfolded right around the time that you were there, and there was another one that was sort of similar, and they were all wrapped up in KHAN primarily and his syndicate.

This the killing at the KIA, at the Kabul international airport, of nine airmen, who had apparently crossed one of KHAN's syndicates, in a corruption scandal. Do you remember much of that?

AMBASSADOR CROCKER: The national military hospital, yes, I absolutely remember that. Again, I believe that was before I got there, but it was the -- the reverberations were still very much around.

Yes, I was -- it was interesting to me that -- and I guess again, it reflects the fear that KHAN could inspire, that would end the establishment, you know, on the part of Afghan military commanders, the chief of staff, the minister of defense.

I don't think I ever can recall an occasion in which an Afghan raised that issue. I think they were probably afraid to, and yes, I do remember the incident at the airport and the -- the view at the time, that KHAN was behind it.

I would have considered him capable of any inequity.

DR. RONDEAUX: How did that complicate efforts to kind of -- to nail it? I mean, you know, there were investigations on both of those cases, and here you had former defense minister, vice president kind of sitting in the midst of things.

But you know, part of the brief politically at that time was to sell the story that we were trying to something about corruption. So, how did that complicate the political picture?

AMBASSADOR CROCKER: Again, that -- all of you know it, some of you really know it, you know, there was a pretty significant US, in deed, international effort on anti-corruption, but you know, just like Kabul Bank, it sadly seemed that, you know, by that time, the corruption was so entrenched and so much a part of the lifestyle of the establishment writ broadly, you know, that I saw little prospect and you know, again, engaged on things like the Kabul Bank, just kind of a sense of utility.

Some of the more discouraging meetings I sat in on were periodic briefs from task force (inaudible), again, with all of the will in the world, and the positivism that has to go with an effort of that sort, I just did not see us making any substantial progress, because it was a systemic issue by that time, which is why, you know, just to reiterate the point again, you know, the corruption lens has got to be in place at the outset, and even before the outset, in the formulation of reconstruction and development strategy because once it gets to the level I saw, when I was out there, it's somewhere between unbelievably hard and outright impossible to fix it.

DR. RONDEAUX: That is true. Well, let me move onto another futile issue that you encountered.

You know, we interviewed Mike MATRINCO {phonetic}, spent some time at his lovely house in Carlisle, he is a true font of wisdom.

I remember him commenting back then, and in probably subsequent conversations that when you first arrived, you said there would be no deal on the bilateral security agreement, that you were discouraged from the outset.

What was it that discouraged you so much about the prospect of a status of forces agreement with the QUASI {phonetic} administration at that time?

AMBASSADOR CROCKER: Which time are you talking about?

DR. RONDEAUX: Well, I guess this would have been in 2011, when you first arrive.

AMBASSADOR CROCKER: Okay, right.

DR. RONDEAUX: Yes.

AMBASSADOR CROCKER: Yes, because you know, I had two charges directly from the President, our President.

One was to get a -- one was to reset the relationship with QUASI and the other was to get a comprehensive bilateral agreement that would involve security, but would go far beyond that.

Yes, at the outset, it was pretty discouraging. Talks had been held in Washington, and they really were going nowhere.

So, we agreed, us in Washington eventually, and the Afghan's, and basically

Washington's view of it was, you know, we just want this off our plate and on your's. So, any way you want to do it is fine with us.

So, we shifted it Kabul, via Washington, so we would have leaders, decision makers right there, and that I'd be the lead negotiator for us. I had done the same thing in Iraq in 2008.

So, you know, once we got that -- once we fixed the structure, I can't say I was fulled with bubbling optimism, I never am, but I could see that we were tracking right, although we didn't know we'd get the deal until we got it.

But in the latter part of 2011 and the early months of 2012, we were on a -- you know, a positive negotiating process. We just had to fix the structure first.

DR. RONDEAUX: Some of the structure, I mean, I was there as well at that time, and I spent a lot of time thinking about, primarily actually, some of the -- the chief hold up seemed to be around things like Bagram and the detainee process, which was -- I mean, at first was not nearly as public, I think, an obstacle as many people understood it to be, who were close to it.

But can you talk about that as an obstacle or a challenge, in terms of the negotiation process?

AMBASSADOR CROCKER: Well, there were several specific problems. Detainees was one. Night raids was another.

The way we approached it was to separate them out from the large negotiation and try to get specific technical level agreements, you know, worked out by people who understood the issues on both sides and to keep them away from the larger political context.

In other words, to de-politicize them, to the extent we could, and you know, we were able to get agreements on both, that a lot of this -- then, to proceed with the larger negotiation and get that agreement.

You know, it was clear to me, from the -- you know, well, not from the outset, but once we -- we had our new negotiating structure, that there was a definite will on the Afghan side, led by KARZI, to get these agreements. It took some effort on our side, to persuade folks that we were not going to get a traditional SILFA {phonetic} and that if we wanted a basis for an (inaudible) presence, we were going to have to be willing to be flexible on points of real importance to the Afghan's, such as detainees, and that we could afford to do it, and again, we were able to get those agreements.

DR. RONDEAUX: How did that -- how did that piece interface with the other piece, which was going on at the time, which was negotiations with the Taliban?

AMBASSADOR CROCKER: Yes, well, there was -- I had a pretty good relationship with Washington. There were issues on which we differed, and one of them was the Taliban.

We paid lip-service to the notion that this would have to be an Afghan led, Afghan managed process, and for me, that is exactly what it was, that my mission and John (inaudible) felt the same for the military elements.

No element -- no part of my mission would get involved in contacts with the Taliban for political purposes, unless we were requested to do so by the Afghan's.

But there were those in Washington who felt that we should try to cut our own deal with the -- with the Taliban, and you know, we had to -- the cutter office surface on my watch.

KARZI was just incensed over that whole thing, and eventually we stood down on that. You know, it really took Secretary Clinton herself, to get a hold of it, and then of course, it re-emerged in subsequent years to, you know, the Taliban deal.

But you know, I was just adamant that we would work this with (inaudible), the de facto head of the high peace commission, and we would do nothing that he did not ask us to do.

But we did undermine our credibility with the -- with KARZI on that issue, as well as others, and then we totally hosed it up later.

DR. RONDEAUX: So, I mean, it seems to me though, you know, you could do business with (inaudible) all day, every day, but if you weren't doing business with (inaudible), you had a real problem.

I mean, there were multiple players at the table, and you know, and this is where kind of the multi-lateral scenario becomes complicated.

The British had their ideas about what the negotiations should look like. The Turks' had their idea. The Saudi's had their idea. The Pakistani's had their idea, and each one of them had their clients inside the national security council, inside the palace.

So, it wasn't just that, you know, your hands were tied. It seemed like it was almost an impossible situation in a way.

AMBASSADOR CROCKER: Well, look, I never believed that the negotiations with the Taliban, conducted by whomever, were going to lead anywhere significant.

I felt at the most, it might be possible

to chip away individual Taliban figures and bring them over to the government side, but that would be an incremental issue.

My concern was managing it in a way that did not do harm to our broader equities there. I never thought there was an upside. I just wanted to avoid the downside, and I could -- I thought involve the downside by dealing with (inaudible) and only with (inaudible) and letting him be the conduit to KARZI most of the time.

You know, if I were -- if I had have taken a different view, if I had thought there was a real prospect to that process, I never believed it.

DR. RONDEAUX: Interesting.

MS. BATEMAN: Excuse me, Ambassador, this is Kate Bateman again.

I wondered if we could just rewind quickly to -- you know, you've alluded, you've reiterated a couple times that with the benefit of hindsight, it would have wiser to have this corruption -- anti-corruption lense earlier on.

But you know, in reality, when, you know, let's say this kind of effort may happen in, you know, Syria, Yemen, Lybia, Somalia next, and with relatively few staff on the ground, when we don't -- we don't have a fulsome understanding of the power relationships, you know, political patronage networks at play, what do you think -- you know, how do you -- do you think that US senior officials have -- currently have some understanding of the importance of considering corruption?

I guess my question is, you know, within the US foreign policy national security establishment, do you think there is now, after 15 years engaged in Iraq and Afghanistan, do you think there is an acknowledgment that corruption is a security -- you know, poses a security threat, a threat to our security goals and our political stability goals?

AMBASSADOR CROCKER: Well, I think certainly for anyone who has worked on either Iraq or Afghanistan, absolutely.

But I'd be very afraid that, you know, when the magical day comes in Syria and Yemen, in Lybia maybe, when the -- the hot conflict has ceased or at least bubbled to a low simmer, that we'll just want to charge in and start fixing everything as fast as we can, because as I alluded to this earlier, it's the American, and that we'll lose sight of what happened in Iraq and Afghanistan, where the ultimate point of failure for our efforts, you know, wasn't an insurgency. It was the weight of endemic corruption. We're going to lose sight of that.

You know, that's -- I'd love to see something our government is not well equipped to do. I'd love to see, you know, the serious scenarios start to be developed now, to establish certain points that what kind of reconstruction efforts might be most vulnerable to corruption and how do you prevent it?

In most cases, probably by not doing it. You know, because otherwise it's just -- it's going to be, you know, January 2002 and March 2003, all over again. Just pumping a whole heck of a lot of stuff into countries that can't manage it, and then, you know, our biggest single project, sadly and inadvertently, of course, may have been the development of mass corruption.

You know, that's the kind of the development legacy, in many respects, and I think there is a chance, based on your efforts and others, to develop a template for a very approach, but you have to start working on it before you need it, and we just don't do that very well.

MR. WASSERSTROM: This is very insightful and thank you very much for these -- these --

AMBASSADOR CROCKER: Yes.

MR. WASSERSTROM: -- thoughts. We keep hearing, and others have said this, this tension between counter-terrorism and reconstruction. Is there a tension between the two?

AMBASSADOR CROCKER: Well, you know, these are huge concepts and undertaking. So, inevitably, one would expect to see elements of tension.

But broadly speaking, I certainly find that, either in Iraq or Afghanistan. You know, the counter-terrorism efforts largely focused on night raids, their own set of political problems as we all know, but in no way, was that amenicable to development. You know, they -- they were just almost literally two different worlds.

So, no, I don't see an inherent tension there, and I -- I was struck reading -- I guess it was yesterday's New York Times, the -- a commander of Afghanistan special forces, talking about how essential the night raids were, that was kind of their whole strategy, and of course, all the, you know, arguments I had with KARZI over that, well, you know, we knew it was an effective tool and it's interesting to have the Afghan's themselves now, saying that it's absolutely critical in our effort to beat back the Taliban, and there is nothing in that again, is inherently contradictory to development.

But here is something that is

contradictory with both development and security. I mean, if you look at the Afghan police now, horribly corrupt organization, and that is retail corruption, obviously.

MR. WASSERSTROM: Yes.

AMBASSADOR CROCKER: Not wholesale.

MR. WASSERSTROM: Right.

AMBASSADOR CROCKER: You know, the Afghan special forces helped by us, can clear an area, but the police can't hold it, not because they're out-gunned or out-manned. It's because they are useless as a security force and they're useless as a security force because they are corrupt down to the patrol level.

Now, I don't mean to, you know, turn this into a pet-rock fetish, but you know, of all the painful lessons I carry out of my time in those two War zones, Iraq and Afghanistan, it's the -- it's the deadlines and corruption at every level, that is the starkest point.

MS. BATEMAN: Sir, if we could perhaps, as one more question. Is that all right for you?

AMBASSADOR CROCKER: Yes, what time is it? Yes, sure.

MS. BATEMAN: About 3:35. Okay, great. The subject of conditionality.

At least in my, you know, slice of time there, I was in -- under -- in Ambassador Rick Olsen's office, and you know, and also before that in SRAP, and I saw this discussion of conditioning our assistance.

You know, there is this great reluctancy to do so, bureaucratically, I think and even just, you know, technically.

What could you say about -- do you see the US -- do you see us as reluctant to actually tie assistance and I suppose first of all, do you see that as a legitimate tool of exerting our leverage?

AMBASSADOR CROCKER: Well, like some of the other tools, it's legitimate if it works.

You know, my sense is pretty well gone over, because of the levels to which corruption had risen and the extent to which they were ingrained, by using conditionality to get rid of corruption just wasn't going to happen.

So, it's -- I thought the approach that we used in the run up to the July 2012 Tokyo economic ministerial, was the right one, which is what would the Afghan Government undertake going forward, to offer donors some level of confidence that assistance would follow the path of previous assistance, and you know, the Afghan's developed the document, pretty much on their own.

That was just shortly before I left, and I remember thinking, well, at least it looks good. Probably will never work, but at least, you know, they did it and it reflects and appreciation on the part of the leadership in Afghanistan, but these are important and significant issues.

But if conditionality is to have any chance, I think in that kind of environment, it has to be generated conditionality. In other words, where the Afghan's come up with their own conditions. Only they will know what is ultimately achievable, you know, not us.

So, externally imposed conditionality, unless you absolutely know what you're doing, which is highly unlikely in these circumstances, probably just isn't going to work.

DR. RONDEAUX: Thank you for your time, sir. You've been very generous. It's quite late. I think we'd like to close, but do you have any questions for us?

AMBASSADOR CROCKER: Yes, just one. Do you -- what is your production schedule?

DR. RONDEAUX: We wish we knew some days, but I will say right now, we have a couple reports that are in the hopper, including the corruption report and the strategy report. We think that at least, you know, by mid Spring, we'll release one or two of them, and then there is another three or four that are kind of also under-scope right now, and those will come out over the course of the next year and a half, two years.

AMBASSADOR CROCKER: Right, and each of these will stand on its own. You're not going to make any effort to extract from them, the few broad general lessons?

DR. RONDEAUX: Well, there may be a Capstone report at the end.

AMBASSADOR CROCKER: Okay.

DR. RONDEAUX: That's still kind of TBD. But at this stage, given also that we also want to be relevant to the current discussions about countries like Syria and Yemen, probably better to keep moving ahead and pushing out what we can, when we can.

AMBASSADOR CROCKER: No, that makes sense, and I hope you will consider a Capstone report, but you know, obviously that's not something you have to decide now.

Well, okay, good luck. I know it's got to be often, very depressing and frustrating, sustained over so many of years by so many of you, but it really is important, you know, as somebody who is on the other side of the aisle here. You're doing important work, and I hope to God it will inform, you know, the next set of nation building experiences.

DR. RONDEAUX: Thank you so much.

AMBASSADOR CROCKER: Thank you.

(Off the record.)

LESSONS LEARNED RECORD OF INTERVIEW

Project Title and Code:	
LL-01 – Strategy and Planning	
Interview Title:	
Interview with (b)(3), (b)(6), (b)(7)(C)	
Interview Code:	
LL-01	
Date/Time:	
10/22/2015; 1030-1145	
Location:	
New Jersey	
Purpose:	
To elicit interviewee's thoughts on U.S. reconstruction efforts in Afghanistan.	
Interviewees: (Either list interviewees below, attach sign-in sheet to this document or hyperlink to a file)	
SIGAR Attendees:	
Candace Rondeaux, Matthew Sternenberger	
Sourcing Conditions (On the Record/On Background/etc.):	On the record. Must approve quotes.
Recorded: Yes [x] No [ ]	
Recording File Record Number (if recorded):	
Prepared By: (Name, title and date)	
Matthew Sternenberger	
Reviewed By: (Name, title and date)	

Key Topics:
- Introduction
- Security Environment
- Rebuilding the Government
- Developing Afghanistan
- Military Cooperation
- DDR and Corruption
- Personnel and Incentives
- PRTs
- International Cooperation
- Brief Tour
- Lessons Learned
- Regional Resources Development
- Follow-up

LESSONS LEARNED RECORD OF INTERVIEW

Introduction

I remember very clearly how I got started. (b)(3), (b)(6), (b)(7)(C) that there would be a packed room with press and thousands of people. I don't think there were 11 people in the room. There was no one from the press. (b)(3), (b)(6), (b)(7)(C) So it was very brief and didn't actually ask me any questions. They gave me some written questions, but it was just the antithesis of what you would expect. Then (b)(3), (b)(6), (b)(7)(C) He had been going back and forth beforehand. So we were there for not very long, a very few days, and then I had to go back to Washington, but I forget for what reason. That was the beginning. I had to deal with him coming and going and he was the one connected with the White House. A lot of this was being run by the National Security Council. It was not my experience of how an embassy normally functions and how the structure functions.

Normally, it functions through the embassy reporting to the Department of State which interfaces with the other components of Washington. In this case, because of the situation, the National Security Council was meeting basically every day about Afghanistan. Lots of things were being done directly by the White House and the National Security Council and Khalilzad was their envoy. It didn't create serious problems, (b)(3), (b)(6), (b)(7)(C)

I would yes and no (b)(3), (b)(6), (b)(7)(C) I was there all the time, he was coming and going. He then got sidetracked into doing Iraq. (b)(3), (b)(6), (b)(7)(C) In this case it was a real circus. I was the one doing that and there was so much going on because this was a very dynamic situation, it kept changing. It was new. This is not the ordinary experience that people had. There was a lot of ad hoc'ism and constantly trying to play catch up through the Washington bureaucracy within the embassy and the situation on the ground. You needed two people there and as you can see, (b)(3), (b)(6), (b)(7)(C). They consistently had a number of ambassadors because this was just a very unique situation and you needed to have a different setup to deal with it. There was an Assistant Secretary that dealt with the refugee population. Bill Taylor was there doing assistance work. I am not sure if he was an ambassador yet. Other people came and went on a kind of ad hoc basis.

The embassy kept growing. (b)(3), (b)(6), (b)(7)(C) Eventually, a few months later we got the famous trailers and people moved into them. We were able to start getting more people in but it was predicated on the number of beds. There was always a line of people

LESSONS LEARNED RECORD OF INTERVIEW

wanting to come. When there was an empty bed then people came. (b)(3), (b)(6), (b)(7)(C) The locals were cooking up goo on the staircase and it was actually better food then when we finally got the cafeteria where they had this American military ideas of what you might want to eat. It was all very heavy and like expanded MRE stuff. I much preferred the local food.

We never lost the embassy compound, the Taliban did a run through just before we took over in Kabul. They knocked in the doors and trashed things up, which provided a good photo op. The building was still there and had been maintained by the local employees during all those years. The same people were there who went through some rough times. For a number of years, we were coming up from Peshawar to pay them, but I think that stopped. So we had this building and I actually have photos of what it looked like in those early days.

So there is a funny story about the trailers. (b)(3), (b)(6), (b)(7)(C)

Security Environment

We had these Marines and it was a real security situation. We had guys with guns on the roof and barbed wire. We only had one real security incident. We did have a number of alarms and things because people were shooting rockets, which you may have heard about. They would go at twilight to the outskirts of Kabul and they would have these kind of high school science project rockets that they would aim in our direction. They hardly ever hit anything. They never hit us, but did hit the NATO compound down the street and started a fire. We made use of our bunkers for that. In 2003, there was a real security incident, and unfortunately it was a predictable one. we had the guards from one of the warlords across the street – I think they were Fahim's people – and I tried from the very beginning to get them out of there. These guys were drunk and drugged. One day they started menacing our guys and pointing their guns at us. Our guys told them to stop and it developed into a fight, and several of their people got killed. We were there and it was kind of a movie thing. (b)(3), (b)(6), (b)(7)(C) It was unfortunate and the Afghan side was apologetic as far as they could be. I think our Marines did the right thing and I told them that. This took place in early spring, maybe March. I remember it was not really that hot out that would be my guess. You can google it as it was in the news. So that was the only incident we had on my watch. They did later have attacks and things, but at the time I was there, things actually looked like they were getting better. When I left in August of 2003, I thought that Taliban would be around, but basically would be nuisance bandits up in the mountains.

Rebuilding the Government

What we have to do is create a situation in which Afghanistan can maintain itself. That was my theme. Before I went out, I asked what we needed to do in order to stabilize? the country now that we are here. I said that for us to be able to do that that Afghans have to be able to feed themselves, protect themselves and govern themselves. That is what I tried to help them do, but that was a time when Washington was saying that we were no doing reconstruction. They did not intend to do that and I did not fight with them being a good diplomat. I just kept slowly pushing in the direction that I thought was correct, which was that we did have to do reconstruction. I tried very hard when I was there, unsuccessfully, to get civil service reforms. So before I went out, I had these three goals. So I tried very hard to meet with Arsala who was the vice president at that time and who was in charge of civil service reform and I tried to get them to do civil service reform. My suggestion, which was never acted upon, was to get the Indians and Pakistanis, both of whom have highly trained bureaucracies leaving aside the corruption and everything else we know that is wrong with them. They do have a system that is in the culture which Afghans

LESSONS LEARNED RECORD OF INTERVIEW

can understand. I wanted them to setup a civil service academy to train people. I thought it would be good for the Afghans learn this and it would be good to make the Indians and Pakistanis cooperate on a project.

It didn't go anywhere for many reasons. First, the Indians and Pakistanis didn't want to be at that tea party. Many people didn't understand the concept. I mean, "let's have bureaucrats" is not a rallying cry that everyone will shout hurrah to. There was a lot of subconscious resistance, because at this time all of the ministries were fiefdoms of various leaders. You can call them warlords if you want or allies if you want, depending how the wind is blowing that day. When you walked into a government ministry then, if you knew your ethnic groups, you could know what ethnic group the minister was from based on who staffed it. They didn't want to give that up. On the local level, everything had been devolved. It is the same problems we have today. It was devolved to the local commanders because of a lack of governmental infrastructure. That is a source of many of the problems that we have today. We are going back to it now with the attacks in Kunduz. The government is saying they are going to rearm the local militias. We have been down this road before.

Developing Afghanistan

I think this is a problem wider than Afghanistan. Just look next door in Kyrgyzstan, we found a relative of the president and gave him the contract for the fuel at our base. A lot of problems erupted from that and we do this over and over again in different countries. I understand the need to keep these people on board and I understand the need not to change the situation or to fold them into something else. (b)(1) - 1.4(D)

This is what happened in France. The aristocracy, as the situation developed, changed and become a filled with factories and mills. Germany went the same way. We didn't do that [in Afghanistan].

As far as oil and gas went, I tried to get a comprehensive survey. I think it was not until 2008 when the [US Geological Service] came out to survey the mineral wealth of Afghanistan. There was talk about this effort even before I went out. We were slow on this uptick. That is part of the problem with things run out of the National Security Council. They were looking at different things. They weren't looking at building an economy. One of the reasons I wanted to rebuild the civil service is that during initial dealings with people in the bureaucracy at various levels, that not surprisingly, they had all been trained in a command economy. I was fortunate, even though I didn't know it at the time that I got to go to the former Soviet Union. I never wanted to go there, but (b)(3), (b)(6), (b)(7)(C)

(b)(3), (b)(6), (b)(7)(C) So, when I went to Afghanistan I saw a lot of things that I would not have known before. One of the things was that the bureaucracy had been trained to think in a particular way. We are all the victims of our schools. I went to catholic school and I will never be able to escape it. That is just the way it is. These people went to the communist school. They realized this in Kazakhstan and they started sending hundreds if not thousands of kids every year to the west to go to university. They thought that if they want to be a modern country and play the game with everybody else, we had to be able to think the way they do. They started thinking in another way. Whereas in Afghanistan they conviction, so they were doing what they thought was good. One of those things was not capitalism. The concept to people in the government is that the government is wise and good and will help everyone. If you allow capitalism, these private companies would come in and make profit. The profit would be distributed to everyone. The idea was that they would pay really good salaries to people and there would be restaurants and people would buy houses. All this would be a downfall from capitalism and that was not something they could compute because it was not a part of their experience. That was a problem and still is a problem for people trying to do business there. They are

LESSONS LEARNED RECORD OF INTERVIEW

having serious problems with dealing with the bureaucracy. They didn't make that ideological change or the way the bureaucrats think.

I was there fairly briefly and it was fairly early on. Later on, Khalilzad brought in advisors from many of the ministries. I don't know how that worked out and it is something that can be good or bad. In one way, you can say this is what the Russians did. They had all these people telling them what to do. The emphasis was on the military, it was not on developing the economy. As I said, Washington was saying that we were not doing state building. We did get them to rebuild the road, but that was something Karzai and I pushed. I said, before I went out, this is a country where most of the people are illiterate, what do you do? I said you do something big that they can see and touch. I said how about the road from Kabul to Kandahar. We built that in near best time and it was a symbol of modernization. I said let's do that again. Karzai had been pushing that independently and it got Washington's attention. So they built the road. Problematic now but for a while it was functioning before the security situation deteriorated. It made a huge difference. Instead of it taking two days to get to Kandahar, you could go in four or five hours. So if you are transporting goods and all the obvious mechanisms, these [roads] are the kind of things that you need. I could not say it was our overall policy. You know the number of civilians only got over 1,000 in 2011 when at a time when we had 165,000 soldiers there. You can stop right there and say we see what the picture is. At that time, there were a lot of security incidents.

In 2002 to 2003, there weren't very many security problems. We could have been everywhere. The people we did have were able to go everywhere. There were constant alarms and (b)(3), (b)(6), (b)(7)(C) not going to lock them up all the time, which is what happened later on. We were going to look at it every day and see what the [security] situation is because you have to get your work done. To my belief, you can't get your work done if you are just sitting at your computer at the embassy. You might as well be back in Washington.

Military Cooperation

There were two sides to this [regarding the varying degree of capacity within agencies to monitor and implement programs]. The one is monetary. If you look at the overall amount of money spent in Afghanistan, you see a tiny percentage of it went to help the people of the country. It almost all went to the military and even most of that money went for local militia and police training. The other thing is that the military was independent of the embassy. (b)(3), (b)(6), (b)(7)(C) That created a logistic problem because it was a 45 minute drive or a helicopter flight. That changed. That was rectified. General Bikenberry at that time in the embassy and he was negotiating with Fahim about building a national army. As far as the fighting was concerned, that was all out of Bagram and run independently. We were informed, more than coordinated with. This all changed. I think that it was good that this was rectified. They brought the generals down to Kabul and it was much closer coordination between the embassy and military. That was a lesson that was learned.

In terms of funding, the overall amount was very small. There is a separate problem of Washington and how Washington functions. This is again, not only Afghanistan, this is true everywhere. The way the government works is that you ask for money for the embassy and you have to produce justifications and submit it. Then in the fall the budget comes out and it goes to Congress to approve it or not. If they do approve it, then they allot the money and it comes out next year. So by the time you get the money it is a year later. Washington allotted $500 million to Afghanistan, but by the time (b)(3), (b)(6), (b)(7)(C) just a couple of months later it had been upped to $1 billion. It was clear that was not going to be enough so we asked for another

LESSONS LEARNED RECORD OF INTERVIEW

$1 billion. We got it, but by the time the money came, [(b)(3), (b)(6), (b)(7)(C)] That is how the system works.

The implications for programming is that by the time the money gets there, you will already need more than that. The priorities of Washington and the programs may change in the meanwhile with the snake pit that Washington is. Everyone is fighting for their own programs and priorities. The people who designed the initial programs may no longer be in place. This is another problem of Iraq and future situations like this. You had this rapid turnover of people. The same thing was true of the military. There is a wonderful documentary that might have seen that was about people, who over three or four years, would visit a village. They would see that they were each learning from the beginning. The new people would be given notes and told to do a job. They would ask which way is north. The same thing was true in the embassy. You had these talented and dedicated people coming but they were only there for a short time.

The programs did not necessarily go away but the parameters of the program may change or the requirements could be different. Or there may not be sufficient money by that time. Is there a government program that does not go over cost? So you might design it for $100 million and then you realize that you actually need is $200 million, so you ask for the other $100 million. By the time the money comes, you need $300 million or you decided that the program wasn't any good – like the schools program. They built all the schools and didn't think about getting teachers for the schools! So you have all of these problems. These are structural problems about how our government works, but just exaggerated in a high profile location like Afghanistan.

When I came in, the people [Afghans] there were people who didn't have experience in government. They didn't know what they were doing. They were new at their job. We were the fairy godmother and just came and gave them all this stuff. We gave them laptops! There were some people who were not ignorant, but just new to their jobs, that thought this [idea of just giving them a lot of stuff] was bad. Everyone always wanted more. To a large extent, at that time, they took what they were given. We tried to explain how it [the U.S. budgeting cycle and the bureaucracy] worked. Later on, [(b)(1) - 1.4(D)] I think you can make a case for a lot of his complaints too. Again, this is a situation that occurs in other places. Look at Iraq and the screw-up there. We just disbanded the army. Did we ask the Iraqis about that? I don't think so. This can happen anywhere and then there is the pushback. When I was in Azerbaijan, I opened the embassy and there was a free election. There was a government of thinking people, who were mostly professors. They immediately started ordering limousines and getting lavish offices. Everyone said, of course, it is human nature.

DDR and Corruption

None of them wanted to give up their perch or their arms for the very good reason that they were afraid it was all going to fall apart again. That had happened several times before. [(b)(3), (b)(6), (b)(7)(C)] Basically, he said that he may need them. No one expected that if they were going to give up their arms that they were going to turn in all their arms. That was the situation in Afghanistan and it still is the situation in Afghanistan. **They had 30 years of civil war behind them. They were not about to turn everything in because the Americans said that this would be a good idea. They were not about to give up what power they had because there was no guarantee that that better day was going to be. They were willing to work it out, but some more than others.** They were weary and still are weary. I saw in the news yesterday that Dostum went up to his area to organize the troops.

They flip flopped and they all have changed back and forth. They will still do that again and through all of the years, everybody was always talking to everybody. That is the nature of Afghan society. Allegiances are tribal and you have to look back in history to see what Europe was like hundreds of years ago. There were feudal lords and they were protecting the people they were exploiting who didn't have anybody else. They betrayed one another and allegiances were constantly shifting. If you look at the fights between the Ottoman Empire and the Austrians, you

LESSONS LEARNED RECORD OF INTERVIEW

will see that there were Muslims on both sides and Christians on both sides. This is the way the world was and this is the way the world still is in Afghanistan. Look at WWII. Germany and Russia were allies until they weren't.

No, [I did not have to grapple with the issue of the black markets and corruption around DDR]. It was just beginning when I was there. It was not in full operation at the time. That kind of leakage is something that happens in every situation. In a world where you don't know what tomorrow is going to bring, you get everything you can for you and yours today. That is true in any country. I don't know if we have learned this lesson [on the leakage of weapons]. It is shocking to know that they didn't know the [serial] numbers of guns they gave out. It was not like the numbers were added on later, they came from the factory with numbers on them. We you gave them out, you should keep track of them. Of course, an ancillary problem is giving them to people who are illiterate who can't read or write. So if people are illiterate you can't keep track of the things. Not everyone was illiterate. I agree with you [that illiteracy was a strawman argument and that the officer corps, which was largely trained in Moscow, was quite capable].

When you are power, you are expected to take care of your own and feather your nest for the time when you are not in power. As far as what we call corruption, yes, it is corruption. Someone in their system who is in charge of something, either (b)(1) - 1.4(D), is supposed to be providing for all of their people all of the time. They come to him because the sister-in-law needs an operation, or want a new car, or want electricity in their house. He is also supposed to provide these things in return for their loyalty. That is part of the deal. That is not just Afghanistan....Tammany Hall. It works in this country too. You take care of your own. Why is our government so dysfunctional? It is because we have everyone in Congress taking care of their own. (b)(1)-1.4(D) was very much like Richard Daley in Chicago. The problem was that he didn't do the other part, which Daley did, of building up the infrastructure and making the city work. (b)(3), (b)(6), (b)(7)(C) **a little corruption is not a bad thing but you have to be functional. That was the part that didn't happen because he** (b)(1) - 1.4(D) **didn't have any experience in being functional. Very few people in the government did, they were appointed to their positions because they were on the right side and they had helped overthrow the Taliban.** There were not that many people who could function. Ghani was one [who could function]. There were effective people there but a lot of the people were not. They did not know how to do those things so they fell back to the bureaucracy that they had which was trained in the communist system.

Personnel and Incentives

No, (b)(3), (b)(6), (b)(7)(C) I don't know what the danger pay was there. I forget what money we were getting. There were people getting various allowances. Anyhow, I how was there and in this kind of situation, since I had been in other situations like it before, the first people don't care if they get danger pay. (b)(3), (b)(6), (b)(7)(C) and it was a similar thing. They just wanted to go there, do that, and be a part of it. It was exciting. Thrilling. I mean everything is included in there. It was a time of war in 2001. You don't ask if you will get an air conditioner in both rooms or only in one room. For the time that I was there, the people who came were entirely dedicated. They just took what they got. Then later on, and this is typical in these situations, people say, ask about how much space there will be in the trailer.

I don't recall it [military remuneration compared to civilians] being an issue. Soldiers were here in the embassy and didn't have to pay income tax, because they were here in the battle. We had to as civilians but I didn't hear any complaints but everyone was aware of it. The State Department is always the little row boat in the ocean with all the big battleships. We kind of never catch a fair deal on these things.

PRTs

They were established [in 2003]. BY the time I left there were about four teams, but only maybe one American team. I think there was one British, German, and Italian one. This was something that the military did, that I didn't get a vote on. I think that they could be useful, it was the Fort Apache [the 1948 movie] aspect of it. **They were** sold as being multifaceted and they would be there to establish a psychological area of security. Within that platform then other people could do their jobs. What happened a number of times was that people come out to do voter registrations or something like that, but then there would be a security issue in the area so they could not be supported to do things. They ended up just sitting in the compound while the soldiers went and did the security thing. Whenever you have something that is multi-use like that, there is always a set of priorities that people have. Naturally, for military people, the primary concern is security. I do think they did some good, but again, they were only just beginning when I was there. I knew some people who were in them later that I worked with in other places. The idea was that perhaps they would evolve into something other, something more civilian administrated.

[The PRTs were commanded by civilians in Iraq and the military in Afghanistan,] maybe that was a lesson learned. Again, I don't know because I was not involved in Iraq, but maybe that was it. At least one of the other teams, I think it was a British team that was led by a civilian. They may have thought about the lessons I just delineated and maybe they just thought it was better to have a civilian in charge or someone who is perceived of being above the fray of the competition of resources. The civilians always come in and say, no, we have to go out and register voters and it doesn't matter if they are fighting on the other side of the hill. The military would say, we have to take care of this and make the area security. The doctors may say, we need to go to the village to treat TB, but everyone has TB. With Lakhdar Brahimi, would go and try to bring all the players together. You need someone like that.

International Cooperation

A part of the problem is that their mandate was weak. It is also how these things are structured. The U.N. does not typically have a mandate to tell people what to do. They have a mandate to ask people to do things and that creates problems. Lakhdar Brahimi was an extremely talented person and he was able to make many people do things. The fact is that each nation approaches a problem in a different way and succeeds and fails in different ways. That includes us. We all have our different approaches. For example, the Germans were given the mandate for training the police. The German idea was to setup a police academy and they would train, over 2 or 4 four years, 400 people to be German police officers. Well, that is great, but Afghanistan needs 10,000 police officers, yesterday. This went around for a long time and you can't step on the German's toes. Finally we worked out a deal, after I was gone, where the Germans would continue to train police officers, but the Americans would train some policemen. It was different can of worms because it was sending out illiterate people who will then turn corrupt.

The Italians were given the mandate for reforming the legal structures and the court system. They had no idea what was involved and that it would involve a wholesale rebuilding of the Ministry of Interior. They had to build police stations and holding places. (b)(1) - 1.4(D) and that would solve the problem. So we had to give them some military attorneys to help draft laws.

We dealt with the militaries and all of their warlords because this is what we typically did, as in going to find these strongmen that will be our buddies. So that is a problem. Every nation had a problem and the U.N. didn't have the power to order people to do anything. The only case I know where they did was in Croatia, in eastern Slovenia when that part came back into Croatia. General Klein was given the mandate; he was made little dictator for a year. He set up his own radio station and he could do anything he wanted. He made it work because he had a very strong mandate and that was very unusual.

Brief Tour

LESSONS LEARNED RECORD OF INTERVIEW

(b)(3), (b)(6), (b)(7)(C) Then I think that he was in Afghanistan for about 2 years, which was short too. Anyhow, a few months one way or another don't matter that much. In Iraq, they also had people there for much shorter period of times and there are good reasons for that. It is extremely stressful and policies are changing in Washington all the time.

Lessons Learned

- **Don't let the National Security Council run the show. Don't let the military run the show.** When [Secretary of State] Clinton came in, she said that we are going use all the levers of the government to manage our relations with the world. I said, well good luck madam. It didn't happen because the others are too strong. The Turks have a saying that all five fingers are not the same. Part of the problem in international relations is that we have not been using all of our fingers. While I was in Afghanistan, it seemed to be going well. The decisions were being made in Washington, but I was on the ground running the day-to-day. The decisions were driven by war. In another embassy that would have been different.

- **Take a long perspective.** This is a systemic problem of our government. We can't think beyond the next election. When we went to Afghanistan everybody was talking about a year or two, and I said to them that we would be lucky if we were out of here in 20 years.

- **Look at the problem holistically.** We treated the problem mainly as a military problem, without thinking about what it means afterwards. We still have this problem today in Afghanistan. How does Afghanistan survive? How does Afghanistan pay for itself? This would have meant developing the resources that they have and getting the geological survey out in 2004 instead of 2008 and then doing some investment instead of letting the Chinese have the world's largest copper mine (which they couldn't do either because of security). It involves a larger commitment than we are mentally able to make.

Regional Resources Development

People were not concentrating on it [mineral resource development]. We didn't have the resources to want to do this. There was one American that worked for a private company that wanted to open a mine in the north. However, you run into multiple barriers including: indifference, lack of understanding on the part of the people who are holding power in Kabul, and the endemic corruption (which make it almost impossible to do anything because everyone wants a share). Plus, the lack of will and intent in Washington. We didn't agree with American businessmen coming in and asking how they can invest. There were some people who came and tried to do things. I mean the Agha Khan, came and built a beautiful hotel that has been attacked twice now. It is not easy to do work there. In Afghanistan, people didn't understand that nobody has to come to Afghanistan to do business. Even though they are very good at trading and business on a certain level, they are not good at production.

As far as oil and gas go, the Russians went away and took their plants and never gave them back. That could have sped things up a lot. That was another issue [the NSC not looking at the regional picture] that I always brought up. I have regional experience. (b)(3), (b)(6), (b)(7)(C) Afghanistan has always been a part of Central Asia. There is a whole dynamic on this. This history is there. Babur, who defended the Mongol dynasty came from Central Asia. He came down to Kabul and is buried in Kabul. There are all of these ties that they all know. Several millions of people in Northern Afghanistan came from Central Asia came in when the Russian Empire drove them south. Yes, they are connected to Pakistan and India, but they are just as connected to Central Asia. The Tajiks on both sides of the border are the same people and are related to one another. They speak the same language. The Tajiks in Tajikistan said that Afghanistan is 100 years behind us.

[We never folded in the regional partners] because of the stupid maps that we draw and because we folded Afghanistan into South Asia. Central Asia is different and holdover from the Soviet mentality. (b)(3), (b)(6), (b)(7)(C)

LESSONS LEARNED RECORD OF INTERVIEW

(b)(3), (b)(6), (b)(7)(C) designate Azerbaijan as place you can speak Russian, Azeri or Turkish. It took a long time because they still think that way. This is true all across Central Asia – we think of it as a Russian world.

Follow-up

You should talk to:

- (b)(3), (b)(6), (b)(7)(C)

LESSONS LEARNED RECORD OF INTERVIEW

Project Title and Code:	
LL-01 - Strategy and Planning	
Interview Title:	
Interview with (b)(3), (b)(6), (b)(7)(C)	
Interview Code:	
LL-01-	
Date/Time:	
October 19, 2015; 14:00 – 16:30	
Location:	
(b)(3), (b)(6), (b)(7)(C)	
Purpose:	
To ascertain the history of reconstruction efforts in Afghanistan, primarily during the first 5 years of the war.	
Interviewees:	(Either list interviewees below, attach sign-in sheet to
SIGAR Attendees:	
Candace Rondeaux; Matthew Sternenberger	
Sourcing Conditions (On the Record/On	On Background - Must contact for quote.
Recorded: Yes x	No
Recording File Record Number (if recorded):	
Prepared By:	(Name, title and date)
Matthew Sternenberger, Research Analyst, 10/28/2015	
Reviewed By:	(Name, title and date)
Key Topics:	

- Early Years – 9/11 to (b)(3), (b)(6), (b)(7)(C)
- Phase Four Planning
- Jumpstarting the Political Process
- Accelerating Success Timeline
- Budgetary Cycles and Planning
- Nation Building and Mixed Messages
- Warlord Strategy and Working with Karzai
- Intelligence Agencies and Pakistan
- Building an Army
- 2006 Review
- Civilian-Military Divide
- NSC Planning Function
- Afghan Reach Back Group
- Foreign Assistance
- Private Sector Development
- Lessons Learned
- Follow-up

Early Years – 9/11 to Joining DOD

(b)(3), (b)(6), (b)(7)(C) DC. I literally got a call on my cell phone from my wife that the attacks were taking place. We [myself and my board] were considering projects to fund the kind of work you see all around

LESSONS LEARNED RECORD OF INTERVIEW

you. ▮▮▮ funded work even in the 1990's on homeland security, on the theory that the enemies in the new period are going to use asymmetric forms of attack. The conversation at the board meeting, when it became clear it was a terrorist attack, went right to that question that proves our hypothesis that asymmetric forms of attack are what are likely to come in the future. Now we have to figure out how to respond and so forth. So it was kind of an analytical response because literally we are in a meeting talk about it literally as it happened. Yes, it was troubling, vindicating. ▮▮▮

[Asymmetric attacks were going to be so pivotal because] we have dominated the upper and middle end of the conflict spectrum with all the major powers were either Russia, just came through the dissolution of the Soviet Union, their defense forces were in disarray. In the early 90's we destroyed the fourth largest land force in Iraq in a hundred hours. The Chinese were coming out of the Tiananmen Square unrest and even the big powers were in no condition to challenge us in the conventional and nuclear levels of conflict. Therefore, any opponent would have to find some other way at getting at us. It would be futile after Saddam was defeated at the conventional level with all the forces that he had, including some WMD at that time. To play at that the level, people would have to find other ways, whether it is terrorism, cyber, counter-space, things like that, that would level the playing field.

(b)(3), (b)(6), (b)(7)(C)

there was thinking about if one does modify the regime or topple the regime, you have to think about what comes after because all of this. The terrorist safe havens and the negative externalities coming out of Afghanistan were products of our not thinking about what comes next, during the Soviet-Afghan war. Those of us who spent a lot of time thinking about Afghanistan in the 1980's and 1990's saw that as an enormous mistake. We could have worked with the Afghans to create a stable post-Soviet situation and that would have precluded the rise of al-Qaeda and all of the other terrorist organizations that took safe haven in Afghanistan in the 1990s. So naturally thinking, if there is going to be regime change after 9/11, to our mind and those folks who lived the Afghanistan problem for a long time, it was second nature to think about what comes next. (b)(3), (b)(6), (b)(7)(C) only when the Afghans are defending and policing Afghanistan, will it not be at risk for being a safe haven. You can get there any number of ways, but you need to get there. That was the probably a minority view right after 9/11. (b)(3), (b)(6), (b)(7)(C)

it seemed clear to me that people weren't fully facing up to that need to create an Afghan capacity that is allied with us, but that polices Afghan territory.

(b)(3), (b)(6), (b)(7)(C)

[The argument was] that you have achieved regime change and that is great and a big step forward and now you have to figure out how to enable our Afghan partners to establish the institutions that will allow them to secure their territory and keep the terrorists out. Obviously, a lot of them just went across the border to Pakistan and they would love nothing better than to return. (b)(3), (b)(6), (b)(7)(C)

LESSONS LEARNED RECORD OF INTERVIEW

[REDACTED]

Phase Four Planning

It [our entry into Afghanistan] happened to fast that I would not have expected them to have Phase IV [plan] on October 7th when the war begins. At one level, they were very forward leaning in that they did the work to do the Bonn process. That was very fast and you have to give Dobbins and Khalilzad and the folks involved in that big credit for being able to move so quickly and also the Afghans that they came to terms with each other - they came together to form the Interim Authority. In my understanding of it, and you will know better than I since you have looked at the documents, that the kinds of things you and I think about in terms of phase four, they were giving to UNAMA. That was sort of the policy decision, whether it was we didn't want to do it or we thought UNAMA would do it better, what have you, but I think that UNAMA was tasked with the institution building and the dividing up roles in the security sector and in other ways. My sense is [REDACTED] that in the course of 2002, there is a sense that the multilateral phase four activities on the civilian institution building is not going fast enough. UNAMA, I think did some things very well, but I don't think it was able to move very quickly on the whole array of institutions building that had to be done. God knows, anyone who is in Afghanistan in 2002 knows that, to say that they [UNAMA] was starting at zero would make it sound too easy. The country had been so destroyed and there was just nothing to begin with. The human capital situation was so dire and so I am not in any way criticizing UNAMA or their people. I think that in the course of 2002 there was greater recognition that if you wanted these institutions and to get building going, there would probably have to be a greater role by us, because at the end of the day, we are the only ones who have the capacity to act on the scale that was required. We have done it in South Korea, we have done it in Europe, and we have done it in Japan. As for any European country, the scale of their ability to act is very small [REDACTED] We are just at a different scale. I think that the 2002 recognition, without being there, is setting the stage for doing more.

Jumpstarting the Political Process

I think that he [Donald Rumsfeld] is a misunderstood figure, maybe sometimes he helps that because he was a little inconsistent on things over time. I think everyone was impressed with the political maturity of the Afghans in the Bonn process and the emergency *Loya Jirga*. Once you see people making political compromises, sharing power, bringing people Ashraf Ghani into be Finance Minister, people started thinking we had more in Afghanistan to work with than we thought. After 9/11 people had the cliché view of Afghanistan of ungovernable, horrific place, never been ruled anyone, tribes, violence, all this kind of thing. They had no perception of the 1950s, 1960s or the pre-Soviet 1970s Afghanistan, which had a function government, institutions and a national army. If the cliché is what you think of Afghanistan, then you would be very reticent about thinking you could achieve much there.

As the Afghans showed some political maturity and bringing in people like Ghani and others who could actually do things in terms of institution building that started to evolve. Where I think

LESSONS LEARNED RECORD OF INTERVIEW

Secretary Rumsfeld came – he said that when he was against the state and nation building, he was against it in the sense of us being the preeminent and dominant force in doing all of these things for people. He was always supportive of programs that helped the Afghans do these things for themselves. Through the time I was involved, he was the biggest supporter of Afghans building Afghan institutions, with our support and our help, but not displacing them and doing it wholly for them…which is an American tendency. He is not all wrong about that concern because it is often easier to do stuff ourselves than to coach people along to do it, given the very low level of human capital after 25 years of war. Now was he always consistent that way? No, probably not, but my entire time I was there, he was the most supportive figure in that respect and put DOD's weight behind the ANA, the ANP program and so forth. I would say that that was what I sensed was his latent position. Others read him as being kind of light footprint, do the least possible, but I sensed he was more interested in helping Afghans build their own institutions than others perceived him to be. The argument (b)(3), (b)(6), (b)(7)(C) was that you want Afghans to defend and police their own territory and be aligned with us. For them to do that, they have to have a government. I called it a minimally decent government that had legitimacy so there were not people other than the extremists fighting it and that people would volunteer for their military. They needed an economy and a revenue system to, over time, make that more self-sustaining than it could be at this particular time. He [Rumsfeld] actually pushed that view Accelerating Success policy review in mid-2003. He was the dominant force at the principal level behind that.

Accelerating Success Timeline

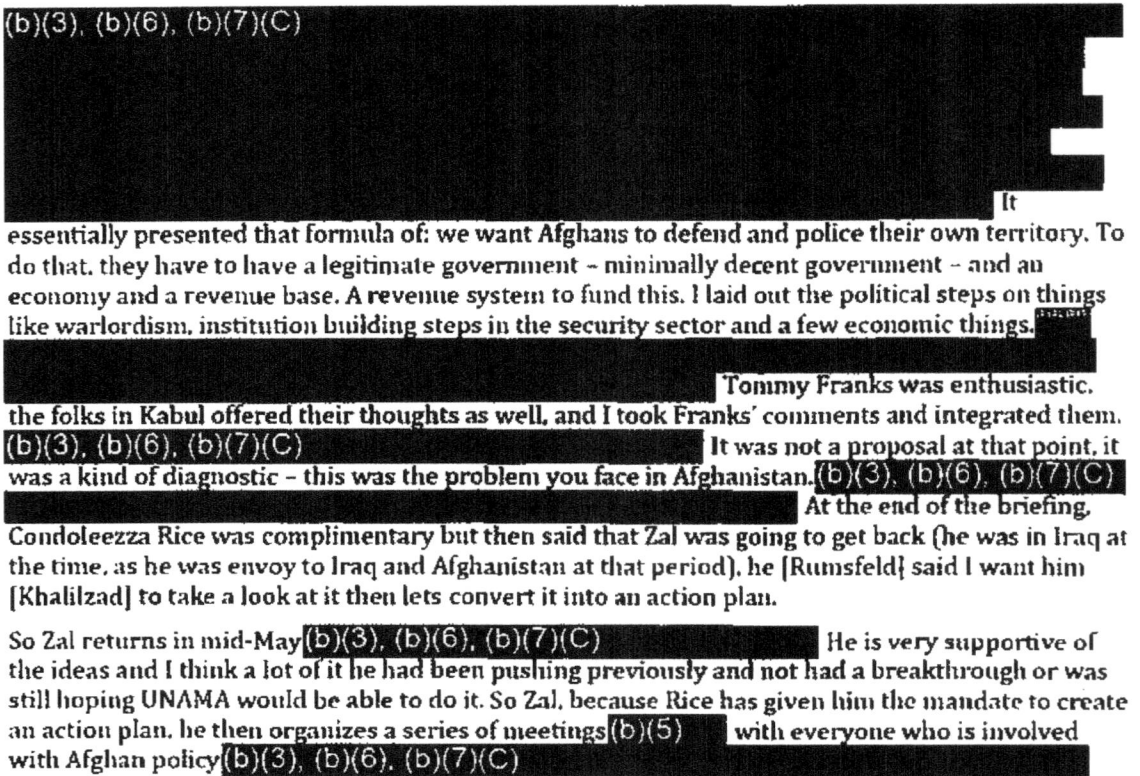

It essentially presented that formula of: we want Afghans to defend and police their own territory. To do that, they have to have a legitimate government – minimally decent government – and an economy and a revenue base. A revenue system to fund this. I laid out the political steps on things like warlordism, institution building steps in the security sector and a few economic things. Tommy Franks was enthusiastic, the folks in Kabul offered their thoughts as well, and I took Franks' comments and integrated them. (b)(3), (b)(6), (b)(7)(C) It was not a proposal at that point, it was a kind of diagnostic – this was the problem you face in Afghanistan. (b)(3), (b)(6), (b)(7)(C) At the end of the briefing, Condoleezza Rice was complimentary but then said that Zal was going to get back (he was in Iraq at the time, as he was envoy to Iraq and Afghanistan at that period), he [Rumsfeld] said I want him [Khalilzad] to take a look at it then lets convert it into an action plan.

So Zal returns in mid-May (b)(3), (b)(6), (b)(7)(C) He is very supportive of the ideas and I think a lot of it he had been pushing previously and not had a breakthrough or was still hoping UNAMA would be able to do it. So Zal, because Rice has given him the mandate to create an action plan, he then organizes a series of meetings (b)(5) with everyone who is involved with Afghan policy (b)(3), (b)(6), (b)(7)(C)

LESSONS LEARNED RECORD OF INTERVIEW

(b)(3), (b)(6), (b)(7)(C)

(b)(3), (b)(6), (b)(7)(C)

So it is approved there, but obviously you then have to get money. So there was contention with OMB about whether we can ask for money as part of the wartime supplemental or the two year budget process and obviously, as I always tell people, if we had gone through the two year budget process we would have needed to know about the need for Accelerating Success several months before 9/11. Eventually Accelerating Success is put in along with the Iraq request. I think it [the Iraq request] was about $40 billion and so Accelerating Success was a small addition. [See here for request] I think that goes to Congress in September 2003. Even before that, Zal was a special Envoy to Afghanistan and starts to execute, so right after the meeting with the President where he blesses Accelerating Success, Zal is on the phone and goes to see the Afghan senior leadership to lay out what we would like to work with them. They are gratified that we are stepping up our effort. Part of Accelerating Success states that it must be a joint action plans with the Afghans because they have to do some heavy lifting too in every domain.

Zal makes a trip in July 2003 to go over that, and then he is back in September 2003 and then October 2003. So on these trips, he is [working on many issues] and one issue was reform of MOD and we had gotten nowhere on that up until that time. Zal gets (b)(3), (b)(6), (b)(7)(C) to work with Eikenberry and reappoint the tier one appointees and then further down the line the tier two appointees. That is achieved at the July trip. So the reform of MOD takes place in September 2003 as I recall. So some of the political components that didn't require money Zal started to implement as part of his Special Envoy position. Meanwhile he is going through the process to be nominated and confirmed as Ambassador, which takes, I think the President asked him in June to be Ambassador and he gets confirmed, I think in early November. He arrives in Afghanistan on Thanksgiving Day in 2003. The money doesn't come into our accounts at the Embassy until about late December. Obviously, if you submit the supplemental in September, it has got to go through Congress. It gets approved, then they have to go borrow the money in capital markets and then treasury gets the money and you know the cascade of money getting to actual spending accounts. It actually gets to spendable accounts in late December/early January.

Budgetary Cycles and Planning

OMB is playing its role. It is the wider architecture that is the problem. In most of the Accelerating Success institution building is either civilian money or money overseen by the civilian side. INL – even if someone else is spending it. The [building of the] ANA at that time was State money given to DOD to do things at the way it was set up way back. You are in that bizarre world for the two year budget cycle. **The civilian side does not have the ability to spend O&M money on something and then go get it reimbursed, which is something DOD can do. So if you have to go**

LESSONS LEARNED RECORD OF INTERVIEW

somewhere right now, you have sort of unrestricted operations money in the DOD money that allows you to do that until you get it replenished in the supplemental. So the civilian side not only at that time had no flexible operations money for anything on this scale, but it also wasn't clear that it had the authority to get serious money through the war supplemental. In that first year, they might have put millions of dollars (maybe in the tens of millions of dollars) might find their way into early supplemental on the civilian side, but not much more than that. So then you are really in a straitjacket. Civilians can't do anything since they don't have those two things the military does.

We haven't done something this ambitious since Vietnam and Korea, in terms of the scale of the undertaking that needed to be done on the state building side. We would go into Panama but would leave and Panama at least still had institutions from before we went in that didn't have to be rebuilt from scratch. We are generally not well set up. So OMB comes along and is essentially operating within the lines, it wasn't willing to help us think outside the lines....or color outside the lines...or re-draw the lines. Dov [Zakheim] might have had frustrations on the military side, I am sure it was nothing compared to the civilian side. Once it was clear that we could put significant money into the war supplementals then you have an improved situation but you still have problems with the legacies - we didn't have train/equip authority, we didn't have CERP yet. There are all sorts of things in the Foreign Assistance Act which impede progress. **If you training the police and under the Foreign Assistance Act, you couldn't actually arm them, because of the old law and things that were done in Latin America in the 1950's.** Once we were trying to build the police force, every police officer only had two bullets. There was inconsistencies that just came from past problems.

The biggest problem that I found, which may be an overstatement and I don't want to speak ill of anyone, but the U.S. government doesn't have any place that knows how to do this kind of planning in the comprehensive way that we came to in Korea or Vietnam. [(b)(3), (b)(6), (b)(7)(C)] **The notion that we have a serious planning capability is a reach. We could conceptualize it, but to do the hard nitty gritty work of costing things and the like, we were at best estimating from folks on the ground.** Then you go to CENTCOM and if you visit the planning folks over there, they have a few other things going on. It is not buildings full of people doing planning at CENTCOM and that point they had Iraq going as well. Their planning capability was severely taxed. AID does not have a planning capability. State does not have a planning capability [(b)(3), (b)(6), (b)(7)(C)] One of the first things we did was to try and create a program tracking cell, the EPIG - the Embassy Interagency Planning Group. It was supposed to help Zal track the implementation of Accelerating Success but also plan next increments of it. **All we could do is plan on an incremental basis.** We could not come to a holistic view of what we needed to do over five years and [for example say] here are the 25 moving parts and here is what it will cost for each of the 25 parts. We tended to plan what we knew. We knew what needed to be done at a conceptual level and then, because implementation capability was uneven, we were always saying we don't ever want to ask for more than we can actually implement. We were working within that incremental planning mode rather than in a holistic planning mode.

It is not so much that [more people] gums up the work, because planning and operations are different. I am sure that those 6 people [at USAID] were probably all ops people. Essentially, you don't have planning.

LESSONS LEARNED RECORD OF INTERVIEW

This was all before S/CRS. Even when it was created, Armitage said that it will not work on Afghanistan or Iraq, which struck us downrange as shortsighted. We would have loved to have some disinterested planning capability to deploy against the problem set. In reading the books about the period, there is a sense that somehow, at that level of State, to become involved in it [in terms of using S/CRS capability in Iraq and Afghanistan] would be to take responsibility for it. If the resources weren't there, you were taking responsibility for something that won't succeed. I don't know if that is true, but that is what is hinted at in the books. Since the President had deployed former envoy to work on this, it seemed to be an administration priority, so therefore you would want to apply skills. I don't know if the capability has been created at State in a serious way or if there is a ground up state/nation-building program.

(b)(3), (b)(6), (b)(7)(C) The civilian mindset at State is not really good at defining the end state and then all the steps to get to the end state. The military is better at thinking that way. It is a project of the culture of poverty in civilian institutions assistance...they will never have the resources to produce an end state and don't think in those terms. The absence of that capability and there is a great book by a young guy named Gregg Brazinsky on our South Korean nation building effort - it is called Nation Building in South Korea. It says that we did very badly after WWII but before the Korean War, then after the Korean War, we were systematic in the rebuilding of institutions, the economy, their military and so forth.

The capacity to think through that is what we need. It is strategically important for two reasons: 1 - if you don't hit the ground and are able to start generating these effects of building institutions, quickly bad things set in. You see this with the criminal networks which take over, warlordism can take root at a deeper level than it would have otherwise, people's belief in the new political institutions wanes and the American people have a limited patience. They [the American people] will give you three years to work on the problem, but if you are not moving fast at three years, and the problems with progress inherent in that, they lose patience. Even in South Korea, Vietnam and other engagements, you have a certain amount of time and then the clock is against you. So if you want to reach success, we need the capacity to start generating effects in partnership with the locals, much sooner than we can under our current system. One of the impediments is the lack of planning capability and the other is the lack of standing forces for doing this. [2-] The military has standing forces, but the civilian side has no standing capability. It can mobilize contractors to do things, but even the mobilization of contractors creates a time lag and contractors can only do certain things.

Also, nothing works without funds. No standing forces and no ability to hit the ground and start generating effects early created negative dynamics in that you pay for it in a big way. If we had anticipated that Pakistan would have helped the Taliban as much as it did to escalate the war in 2005-2006, and if we had been smart enough to essentially adopt the Obama ANSF program, right from the outset, we would have precluded the ability of the Taliban to escalate. We would have reached the 352 [thousand] number by the time the Pakistanis were ready to escalate. That time lag of our recognition, mobilization, and then producing the ANSF that Afghanistan needed, puts you way behind the ball and helps the enemy in a huge way. It creates opportunities for the enemy that once they have escalate it is so much harder to overcome. These are strategic consequences to this. This is not just doing good or it would be nice to be able to operate better. You succeed or fail on whether you can do these things in a timely manner.

LESSONS LEARNED RECORD OF INTERVIEW

Nation Building and Mixed Messages

I agree on the mixed messaging [toward nation building at the outset] very much. I don't think that was ever overcome and that comes from the President as well. Sometimes he is talking about a Marshall Plan for Afghanistan and sometimes he is kind of validating his pre-government rhetoric about becoming involved in these sort of things. It [mixed messages] definitely hurts. If you look at the period, every budget submission, every supplemental, is building the amount that we are doing and I don't remember (between regular budget and supplementals) we are up to $4-5 billion by closeout time there. The mixed message is debilitating in some ways, but the positive side of the mixed messages is also at work. Far better if we operated the way we did in South Korea after the Korean War. Everyone just understood that we have to stand up the South Korean institutions, their military, their police, their education institutions, and their economy. I also like to remind people that South Korea, by every social indicator was worse off after the Korean War, than the Afghans were after the Taliban. The devastation of the armies moving up and down the peninsula, plus the Japanese occupation previously, it was a comparable situation, but we were systematic in one, where we were mixed message in the other. **The mixed message prevents you from being systematic, even if every year you are doing more and better things. The mixed messages hit the most because everyone had the mentality that we would be done in a year. Everyone was just thinking in terms of what we could do in the short term or the short/medium term. No one was saying that it took South Korea 20 years to go from an absolutely devastated place to an Asian Tiger. There is no short cut. You have to work hard for those full 20 years, both the locals and their supporters. It is so inadequate what we are leaving in place.**

The mixed message was even worse under President Obama because he speaks with almost contempt of nation building. Everybody hears that. In our bureaucracy, they hear it. The Afghans, they hear it. People behave on the basis of it. The military hears it, they become more kinetic instead of the right blend between kinetic and not kinetic. This is not to say that lots of things weren't done well during the Obama period, but that rhetoric, I think very harmful.

Warlord Strategy and Working with Karzai

In the original briefing to Rumsfeld, there was a discussion of the need for a legitimate government. Warlordism was a mortal threat to the legitimacy of the regime that we were helping to establish for many reasons, including the abuse of the locals by the warlords. **These were the very people that made the Taliban seem like a good alternative to Afghans in the mid-90's.** So the **Warlord Strategy** is essentially to engineer a series of deals with the warlords in which they would agree to demobilize their private armies in exchange for some kind of political role in the government – provided they would operate by the rules of the new Afghanistan.

MOD reform is really the first implementation and important in and of itself. It is part of the warlord strategy as it is moving the MOD from being essentially one faction's MOD to start to reshape it into a national institution. [An institution in which] different regions and different political groups are represented in the senior leadership. As the reform went down through the ranks in terms of the different ranks of MOD, you're doing everything to create a national institution rather than a factional institution.

The next action was when Sherzai was moved from Kandahar to the Ministry of Urban Affairs in September. That essentially was the first one of these deals that was worked out. Then in October there was a crisis where all the Northern Alliance (if you include Dostum, who was always ambiguous about his inclusion in it). There was a sense that the warlords were essentially

LESSONS LEARNED RECORD OF INTERVIEW

conspiring against Karzai. And Zal went there for a trip. He [Zal] sat down with all the people [warlords] and said that if they were acting against the Bonn process that we can't work with you. He then negotiates the **October Governance Agreement**. Zal took all the heavy lifting items, such as Accelerating Success and DDR and had Khalili (the Vice President) mediate a negotiation which all the principal figures, including the Northern Alliance commanders agreed that this was the path to be taken. There would DDR, there would this, there would be that. That was all agreed in October and Zal uses that to push forward on dealing with DDR and separate political deals with other warlords.

The notion is that you are going to work on the warlords and the DDR while you are building up the capacities of the ANSF and the police. You don't want a vacuum, but bringing one down without the other coming up. The police program was one that could be carried out relatively fast based on the State Department's plan they put forward. In the course of 2004, I think that three quarters (of whatever the number was at that time) would be trained by mid to late 2004 with the 8 regional training centers that Dyncorp would setup and run with the MOI. I think the ANA would also reach like 15,000 by mid-Summer or early fall of 2004. The judgement was that, as that was getting to those levels, than DDR'ing militias would not leave a vacuum. That is the theory and I am sure it was not perfect in practice. You see a series of deals with folks in Jalalabad and in northern Afghanistan in the course of late spring and summer. Ismail Khan being the last one after the conflict with Amanullah Khan in the west. That was all part of the strategy on warlordism. People would critical in some sense for keeping these people in government. My view and I think Zal's view and the others in the Bush administration was that when they don't have their private armies that is good in and of itself. You can then deal with them if they continue to misbehave easier than if they did have their private armies.

The first level of DDR was for the cantonment of heavy weapons. These were really impressive heavy weapons stores. when they brought the Luna missiles through Kabul from the Panjshir Valley. These were not scuds, they had Luna missiles. When you went up to see Dostum's cantonment area – these were serious armories of stuff. I think that people who diminish what was achieved in this phase are a little unfair. **The elimination of private armies was an important political milestone to normalizing the country's politics.** This is not the end point and if the government does not watch over these people they will not behave well.

One thing people underestimated in Afghanistan is how much these figures desperately wanted to be close to us and to be seen as close to us. Part of their power derived from that. That gave you enormous political influence to make demands of them.

They know that Afghanistan on its own is finished. Therefore, you had an ability to do things politically, that you didn't, for example, in Iraq. In Iraq, everyone preferred their local regional partners to us. In Afghanistan, everyone preferred us to the potential local supporter. The **Warlord Strategy** was premised on that influence relationship and the capacity to work step-by-step and never pushing change than could be achieved peacefully. In the course of 18 months, according to the UN reports, a lot was DDR'ed. A lot was also built up to avoid the vacuum by creating the ANSF. That was the theory.

In an ideal world, we would be able to in one fell swoop go from troublesome and negative political actors to positive wonderful civil society actors. The only way you could have done that would have

LESSONS LEARNED RECORD OF INTERVIEW

been with a very heavy footprint. The level of knowledge you need about a foreign society to carry off a heavy footprint without the friction of your presence alienating people would be very high, especially for a place as complex as Afghanistan. I think the ease with which people would make mistakes and be used by one local actor against another would be very high. To me, there was no ideal solution. The phased effort to me was the least bad option. It does have its downsides.

Again, the mixed message of it all is that after Zal's time there, no body polices the bad actors. We step back and say it is all up to the Afghans now. Karzai was a very effective person in proving the quality of Afghan political circumstance. When he had close working relationship and trust with us. We did do things like Sherzai, the October Governance Agreement, Dostum, Atta, and all these things with him. He took risks as long as we planned on how to cover those risks with him before we embarked on any of these courses of action. Once he is on his own and once, over time, trust is broken, between Karzai and us, he doesn't want to be out there on his own. (b)(1) - 1.4(D)

Intelligence Agencies and Pakistan

(b)(3), (b)(6), (b)(7)(C)

What you do find across all cases, everywhere, that these post-conflict, post-civil wars is that there is an externality of completely pushing someone out is that they tend to create organize crime networks. You see that happening in Afghanistan as well. (b)(3), (b)(6), (b)(7)(C) We cleaned all the people out of the military and stuff but they just created organized crime networks with their old people. I tell people that it is not that you have an answer that you will have no problems with, you can choose though what problems you will have next. It will be a phased effort if you are going to help a country like that. It won't be one fell swoop. (b)(3)

(b)(1) - 1.4(D), (b)(3)

This will be a combination of things (b)(3), (b)(6), (b)(7)(C) When Musharraf gives us the ability to operate through Pakistan to knock down the Taliban regime, there is a view as it is said by all of the principals, that Musharraf and Pakistan are our most important ally in the War on Terror. Because of people's personal confidence in Musharraf and because of things he was continuing to do in helping police up a bunch of the al-Qaeda in Pakistan. There was a failure to perceive the double game that he starts to play by late 2002, early 2003. You are seeing the security incidents start to go up and it is out of the safe havens. I think that the Afghans and Karzai himself, are bringing this up constantly even in the earlier parts of 2002. They are meeting unsympathetic ears because of the belief that Pakistan was helping us so much on al-Qaeda. So to what degree is there a recognition of this and by which principals? It varies and you would have to go person by person, but there is never a full confronting of Pakistan in its role supporting the Taliban, Haqqani Group and Hekmatyar ever. (b)(3), (b)(6), (b)(7)(C)

LESSONS LEARNED RECORD OF INTERVIEW

(b)(3), (b)(6), (b)(7)(C)

Building an Army

In Accelerating Success there is a component on the ANA. The argument at the time among the Afghans and us was about what the numbers needed to be. The people like (b)(1) - 1.4(D) were arguing that since we live in a tough neighborhood, the ANA has to be 200,00 in order for us to defend ourselves against the irregular and regular threats in our neighborhood and to deter them – you prefer not to fight. There were other Afghans like (b)(1) - 1.4(D) saying we can't afford a force of that size; those most we can afford is something like 50,000. The affordability versus the requirements to the neighborhood was the big argument at the time. **The way it gets resolved is the way everything gets resolved in Washington – by not getting resolved. In Accelerating Success the goal is to build up to 70,000.** At that time the force because it was under Fahim and no one was volunteering to join because it was a factional army. People were saying that as soon as we were in the neighborhood of 70,000 then we think about if you need more. The great thing about MOD reform was that we suddenly had volunteers than we could cope with.

Barno, and, I think, Major General Westin, rejiggered things and reallocated monies within what we had. We then asked for more in the next supplemental to pick up the pace of rebuilding. Even then, the long problem was not Afghans volunteering, but places to put them. We didn't have basing, barracks or all these kind of things. We were putting people in tents and so forth. The question of getting the program synched up to build quickly to 70,000 and then beyond takes most of 2004-2005 period. It is bumpy that way, but there is a recognition that we will look at the number again as we are building toward it. Ultimately, every time we get near the targets, it gets increased because the security situation warrants it. There is a third issue of quality and if you build too fast you build too fast will you lose the quality? All legitimate questions, but if we were well positioned to do this kind of thing, we would be able to build rapidly and with quality. On the military side, even with all their capabilities, all the organizations that do this sort of thing are ad hoc – there is no MINSTICKI (MINSTC-I) in a box, which you send and it folds and it starts training people. I always argued that a MINSTICKI in a box is just as important as having artillery. There should be standing forces that know the science and are ready to deploy to train indigenous forces quickly.

We have the ANA slide [in Accelerating Success] and there was another slide that dealt with the "strategy for the south and the east." We saw that there was an incipient insurgency there and Barno was going to shift us from counterterrorism posture to a counterinsurgency posture. So if you talk to him, he can take you chapter and verse. He arrived in October 2003 and before that we had most of our forces in Kandahar and Bagram. We would deploy on sort of equivalent modern day search and destroy missions looking for high value targets. When he [Barno] arrived he redeployed that capability to small firebases and PRTs in the contested areas to create relationships with locals and also to cooperate with the ANSF as they start to be trained and deployed to these areas. It was to create the locally deployed force that can work on securing contested territories. There was also a slide that softly addressed the Pakistan problem. It walked about the need for creating a regional conditions conducive to the stabilization of Afghanistan. That took recognition of the problem, but the challenge with us was in the interagency.

LESSONS LEARNED RECORD OF INTERVIEW

There was a different set of people that dealt with Afghanistan policy than dealt with Pakistan policy. So we couldn't dictate Pakistan policy in the Accelerating Success basket, but there was some work done in terms of an intelligence review of the Pakistan problem mid to late 2003 that documented the nature of the problem. **Talk to General Vines.** He and others who worked in Vietnam know what a sanctuary does to you. They, Vines and McNeill were aware of this problem and, I am sure through military channels, raising it. **It was definitely part of the zeitgeist for people dealing with the Afghan policy in 2003, but we don't control Pakistan policy. The level of people fashioning Accelerating Success, we could only focus on Afghanistan. At the principal level there was a view on Pakistan and Musharraf specifically, that made it challenging to introduce the issue. When you are not even willing to raise an issue, you certainly have not exhausted your means.**

(b)(3), (b)(6), (b)(7)(C) Probably the most important thing to do is undertake a mediation between Afghanistan and Pakistan to address their historic issues. At the end of the day that is what Pakistan's bad conduct is driven by and we never truly tried except a couple of trilateral meetings that were not very well prepared and didn't go very well. I don't think we ever took a run at that. [There were costs for Karzai]. If you told him that we understand the problem but we can't deal with it right now or that our priorities are al-Qaeda, he would understand it. I think a lot of the time we told him that there wasn't a problem when there obviously was and that undermines trust. I that that is true [that he felt abandoned] and that comes after Zal leave. Khalilzad had the ability to work with him on that problem in a way that [Ambassador Ronald] Neumann does not. The way to work with Karzai on a governance problem like that is to sit down with them and spend countless hours talking with him until there is a common understanding of the problem, then kick around ways to solve it politically without violence. One solution the entails him taking certain actions with risk, and us taking certain actions that covers those risks, then moving out on a collaborative course of action. You could enormous things with Karzai in these very difficult things, with far fewer resources than we had later. But if you are not will to engage in the collaborative problem solving and covering the risk of the enterprise, he is going to cut deals (b)(1) - 1.4(D) That is was takes place after Khalilzad redeploys to Iraq. The succeeding Ambassadors' line was that we would return to being a normal embassy. We were not a normal embassy in South Korea for a long time. Khalilzad had a line – as soon as it is a normal country, it will be a normal embassy.

2006 Review

LESSONS LEARNED RECORD OF INTERVIEW

[(b)(3), (b)(6), (b)(7)(C)]

Civilian-Military Divide

The first thing that has to happen is downrange. When we operate in something like this, there needs to be unity of command, not unity of effort. So if it is a situation there is a lot of lead flying in the air, it makes sense for the general of whatever task force that is deployed to be in charge of both the military and civilian elements. So the ambassador would essentially be his chief political officer. He should be able to give orders to that chief political officer just as he would another subordinate. Similarly, if it is more a stabilization operations and there is not as much lead flying in the air, the military should be put under the ambassador as it nominally was in Vietnam since it was a military assistance command in Vietnam. It was technically under the ambassador. **Our current system works if you are lucky and you get a Khalilzad and Barno or a Petraeus and Crocker, where for some reason they all agree on the priorities and work well together. They are in sync. That is basically luck. For every one of those you have a Bremmer and Sanchez, or Eikenberry and someone else. Unless you have unity of command, this kind of stuff doesn't work.**

If you are operating on the scale of Afghanistan or Iraq, certainly a Syria, the train and equip thing is such a huge undertaking that only DOD can do it. **DOD has a scale of operations, the logistics, the capacity to procure what you need to procure and all the rest. You need multiple orders of magnitude greater than a civilian agency. The only way a civilian agency can operate, even at a modest scale is through contractors.** [(b)(3), (b)(6), (b)(7)(C)] in Afghanistan, INL had, I think, two people in the embassy overseeing the Dyncorp regional training program. Loved the two people, they were great people, but it is just two people. Compared to what CSTC-A, you just are not in the same league. If it is the scale of rebuilding large forces from nothing, it has to be DOD because nobody else knows how to do it. DOD, in turn, has to have standing, skilled capability in that domain. It is equivalent of another combat arm. **You wouldn't invent how to do infantry operations at the start of a war. You wouldn't invent how to do artillery at the start of a war. You have a skilled capability that train at it and there is a science to it. Similarly to building indigenous security forces, you need the science behind it and people who think about it 24/7 and who deploy and do it as well as our military does other combat operations. Right now, it is all ad hoc. There is no doctrine, no science to it. It gets done very unevenly. When you are creating security forces for another society, it is the most important political act you will ever do. That requires an awful lot of thought and sophistication to create a force that will support the political order rather than undermine it.** If you are doing it ad hoc, sometimes you will have very smart political operators, primarily military, but other times you will not. What you can be doing can be counterproductive to the long term progress of society. **Only DOD can do it, but DOD needs to see this as a core mission and to have dedicated force structure to undertake it.**

I guess seeing INL operate, I think INL you can do if there is an existing police force and if you are doing light level training or capability enhancement, or liaison, that is within their capacities as an institution. Everything else would end up being done by Dyncorp anyway. Unless INL becomes a different organization (not a contracting organization), but an operation organization, I don't think you could ever give them the tasks of the scale you mentioned. It is hard to do this stuff.

There are ways to blend it. I remember in Afghanistan there was a year-long struggle over the question of if INL would stay in charge or if it would get shifted to CSTC-A (or whatever it was

LESSONS LEARNED RECORD OF INTERVIEW

called at the time). There was a man running INL, who was backed by Armitage. Rumsfeld wanted to take on the training of the police because he say the importance of the police. Barno and Zal had developed a supped-up program to take it to the next stage after having down the regional training centers. They wanted to do similar things like the reappointment of tiers of command in MOI like that had been done in MOD. They even went so far as to say that INL will be in CSTC-A, but the pinnacle of CSTC-A for this program will be an INL person. This means you will be in charge of it and give it the strategic and political direction if you are worried about our capacity to do that. We will give you DODs logistical, manpower capability to serve the training of the police. Even that was not good enough. It was only when Secretary Rice took over that the authority transfer took place. I think they still kept an INL person in the lead. If there is talent in INL for this kind of herculean task, there are ways to transplant it into a DOD structure if there is a unique civilian skill in knowing how to do this that has to be tapped. I don't think that since the U.S. government doesn't have a national police force, creating the people who can enable and lead this kind of a project is a task unto itself.

[Transferring authorities into DOD] is a question of scale. The president decides. [You tell the President] the context and ask if he would rather have the DOD doing this or State doing this. That is the kind of determination that the president should make with the NSC arguing it whichever way they want. There are some settings where State would be perfectly good, but in your Syria example, which started the conversation, there is no way but that DOD can do it [Syria] because it will be so chaotic and so violent. It will be so enormous a task that is unlikely to be built or done by any other organization. Again, if you have some absolutely brilliant leader in State – just appoint them over to lead whatever CSTC-A equivalent you create. The president can do that. The president can put a civilian in the military chain of command anywhere he wants. He doesn't need authorities to do that.

NSC Planning Function

My general reading of history is that you can't protect a president against themselves. I am a huge fan of the Eisenhower NSC system. **Even though their structure was more designed to think about long term strategic competitions, like the Cold War, there is no reason that an element of the strategic planning side this NSC couldn't be the repository of this kind of contingency-based lessons and choices. Essentially you are trying to give the president a decision assist tool.** The consequential nature of not having it was evident in Libya. If the problem was that the Bush administration actions had inadequate thinking about the post-war circumstance, the Obama administration took it to having affirmatively no thinking about the post-war. That was a chosen course of action. Everything that happened in Libya was predictable based on the problems of Iraq, Afghanistan and Bosnia. Just having something at the NSC that says, "Sir, if you go down this path, this is what history tells us Libya will look like in 6 months, 1 year, 2 years...it will be Somalia." He can then reject that if he wants. It sure would be good if there was that – the Eisenhower strategic planning side of the NSC would confront the president with those choices. Reading history...you go to war with the president you have, not the president you wish you had. It shows how our system is designed to sewn in power to the civilian leader. You get the pluses and minuses of what that particular individual understands and doesn't understand.

Afghan Reach Back Group

There is a DOD thing and a State thing. **We had a small embassy that was not big enough to do analytical work or to solve analytic problems. So we wanted a group created and composed of all the interagency people who work on Afghanistan all day, every day.** The embassy

LESSONS LEARNED RECORD OF INTERVIEW

would be able to send back a problem that we were up against and ask for the group to work it and present some options or suggestions of a solution. **It never worked that well.** It became the equivalent of the PCC. It became an organization that served the deputies, rather than something that served the embassy [REDACTED] for some solution to the problem that we were training the police, but we can't arm them or get them ammunition. [REDACTED] that problem back to them in late 2003 and 6 months later, they came back and said there is no solution to this because of the Foreign Assistance Act. **They were good people and tried to help us with the problems, but it didn't become that natural cooperative relationship where people in Washington could work Washington problems or do analysis of things or suggest how it was done elsewhere.** It was supposed to support the embassy. When you are on the ground, as you all know, things are moving so fast and you can't keep up based on all the competing demands of the bureaucracy and they can only give you a fraction of their time because they have lots of meetings to attend to and the priorities of their principals to attend to. It [AIOG] was at best, a modest help. It actually improved connectivity so there was probably a better understanding in Washington as a result of that connectivity, but it was not the reach-back support that was envisioned.

The DOD one, run by [REDACTED] participated in the AIOG, but it tried to help us on DOD problems and to help recruit for the Afghan Reconstruction Group and to get the ARG people through the State personnel system which not an easy task. They did help because they could solve DOD-based problems and they did help staff the ARG. [The group was] mainly high subject matter experts and if we were trying to work on infrastructure problems, construction, electricity – having people who have done that sort of thing in the private sector; people who knew more about it than those who were in government about stimulating private sector development. Those would be ARG people. One of the best people we ever had was a fellow from Treasury who work with the MOF on improving their systems and capabilities based on knowing how Treasury works. It was senior subject matter and functional expertise because when State staffs an embassy you have the Ambassador and DCM who will both be senior. The political counselor will be a step down then it is working level and often very young people and they can't give you that subject matter expertise. Same with USAID. You will often have very good mission director and then good next level folks, but then it gets very young, very soon. This gave you more senior expertise in the different domains.

There was one guy on Agriculture in all of USAID that was a senior agriculture expert at the time when we were thinking about agriculture. USAID used to be great in the 60's and 50's in these domains and had big league talent in some of these domains, but now it is assumed that you will get a contractor to bring expertise into the picture.

Foreign Assistance

We should rewrite it [the 1961 Foreign Assistance Act] from scratch. It is a completely barnacle encrusted thing. It is inconceivable that we couldn't do better today. I think that also, in the entire USAID domain of institution building and development, I would look toward CORDS model in Vietnam. **Everything we do (a critique also made by Ghani) is create parallel structure and then hire away all the talent from the government for our contractors and NGOs and our other implementing partners because we pay them so much more.** I think that there is a lot of truth to Ghani's critique so to me the answer is how could you do, in this kind of contingency, restructure ourselves so that we are actually supporting the creation of an Afghan institutions and firms. CORDS, historically was the best case of that. The parallel chains [of CORDS] and the ability to spend counterpart funds in kind. We had counterpart funds that were not treated

LESSONS LEARNED RECORD OF INTERVIEW

like tax payer dollars, because if you are going to spend taxpayer dollar in Afghanistan, all the accounting requirements that come with it make it impossible to do it through an Afghan institutions. If you have counterpart funds you can put them into Afghan institutions and if you have the parallel chain of command that CORDS had, they can have oversight in a direct way but not at the level of USAID accounting practices. By spending money through Afghan institutions with oversight, probably jointly working contract and bidding process with them too. We have put a western American talent into strategic planning and the procurement offices of ministries or provincial governments, which was easily doable through a CORDS structure, then you could get a high degree of accountable, but not western style/USAID accounting. It would be sufficient that you would be confident that you are not throwing money away. Yet, **it would be Afghan institutions that would be doing these things and you would save an enormous amount of the 50% overhead that spend on western contractors and then the cascade of overhead rates that all their sub-contractors take to where you have almost nothing being spent on the ground in some cases.** For these type of contingencies, redesigning it all through a CORDS-like mechanism is far preferable to our current system of parallel institutions and western contractors with their overhead rates.

The inventor of PRTs, Dan McNeil, served in CORDS. It is kind of an echo of them, but without the full system that made CORDS work. If you work at the 1971 National CORDS Strategy, everything that was done down to the district level for every district in Vietnam was specified in the plan. You had the capacity to implement the plan and oversee it because of the CORDS structure because of all the parallel offices that accompanied the program. Unless you put those things in place, you don't get the CORDS affect. Some of the PRTs were close to provincial governments, so in a limited way you kind of had that, but other times PRTs themselves were parallel to the provincial government. In the early years, it was more the latter than the former. Over time, there was a greater consciousness with working with the local goverornment.

[The French operations in Indochina did not decimate the human capital, whereas in Afghanistan you didn't have that.] When you get down to the district and village level in Vietnam, you are essentially working with society. Just as PRTs went to a village they were working with society. The Afghan government begins and ends at the district level. There is nobody in the villages [from the government]. **I think that if you were doing systematically, one of the first things you would put on the ground would be a capacity to start training district administrators.** No one was ever that systematic. They either sort of generate on their own or they don't generate. How hard would it be to train 407 people [one for each district] in the early years just to get things happening? Everyone always argues unitary systems, not you need an entire system. The people who argue a unitary system was a mistake underestimate the problems of provinces and districts that have different ethnic or tribal groups in them. Whoever wins the election gets everything and the others feel downtrodden and the notion of the central government appointing someone of neither. Who had that training program? Nobody had it. Then you get the IDLG trying to find people to put down there [at the district level], but wouldn't it have been better if there was an ANA-like program for that?

We tried to work with Jalali when he got there to ramp it up but improving that side of MOI through the MOI reform that would have been the next stage of things, but it would have been better to have had that from day one, but we didn't.

Private Sector Development

LESSONS LEARNED RECORD OF INTERVIEW

No, [we are not good at private sector development]. Yes, it was a post-Soviet country, but basically nothing from the Soviet period survived so I am not sure apart from that fertilizer plant up in Mazar, I don't remember seeing anything standing or some former state farms in Jalalabad. In a setting like this, it was very different from Saddam where you could have restarted a lot of things that existed. **First, USAID doesn't even want to deal with private sector development. The one thing that we tried to get in Accelerating Success was an enterprising fund, but I think USAID conspired with their friends on the hill to kill it because they just don't like private sector development. We struggled to even have them do a contract with the Afghan Ministry of Public Works to pave a road so that we built local capacity in their road building world instead of just giving a contract to Berger that would give it to a Turkish firm and so forth. We don't have a structure that wants to do private sector development so it is very unlikely you will be able to do it.** Their mindset is much more on like working on literacy or the thirty year development goals, which is good as we are for primary schools and I am glad for that. Afghanistan has certain potential sources of wealth – agriculture sector, regional trade, or the mineral sector. I always argued that we should work with Afghans to create sectoral development plans in these areas where they have historically, and by current analysis, a likelihood of being able to develop a thriving sector and exports. USAID has no notion of how to do that…maybe in the agriculture area, they will hire a contractor that will help people do better at their subsistence farming than they are doing now. (b)(3), (b)(6), (b)(7)(C) Let's say you look at Afghan agriculture and the soil and the climate here is ideal for high value added spice development, as it happens to be. Why don't we get McCormick to come over here and we will actually pay you to create the entire value chain for the spice subsector of Afghan agriculture. So you go teach the farmers how you grow these spices to be able to produce for world markets (quality, grading). Then you create some Afghan firms that will buy from the farmers and package and create the value added goods and all the way through the value chain to sending things to world markets. You [McCormick] will make money because you will be involved in this value chain at various parts, you may actually be the guy who gets it in the end. We will give you money to create the Afghan value chain because you know how to create a spice value chain and no one else does. USAID doesn't know it and DOD doesn't. You do it all over the world so come do it in Afghanistan. SO that creating the value chain, by having a private sector actor that is the world expert struck me as an appealing model, but that is not a model that works with USAID.

Similarly, we had to go to USGS to hire them to do the mineral survey. That was a State idea in Accelerating Success. (b)(6), (b)(7)(C) was the Afghan Coordinator at the time [for State]. It was not USAID, it was State that brought that in. Barno volunteered the helicopters to fly the survey instruments around and an ARG expert who had been a deputy minister of mines and minerals in the pre-Soviet Afghan government, was involved in doing that as well. If I were going to develop the Afghan mineral sector, having the expertise of an American mines or minerals organization to create the value chain and help the Afghan firms get stood up and train their personnel. Otherwise, it essentiates luck. So that sort of private sector development – maybe we have done it sometimes, possibly the agriculture domain in the Ukraine. We just don't function that way in USAID. I am huge believer of Hernando de Soto that property rights are important and the way USAID does property rights doesn't work. It is very hard to do because all of the corrupt elites of the world know that keeping property rights out of the hands of normal people is a good way to maintain their dominance over them. De Soto was successful in Peru, but not helpful in helping people in other

LESSONS LEARNED RECORD OF INTERVIEW

countries cross the threshold of actually implementing the formalization process that worked in Peru.

You are absolutely right [that property rights is tied to inheritance and one must look at dominant schools of thought in each area to adjust the inheritance system appropriately] and the added complication in the 25 years of horror the number of regimes that gave away the same land to different people or faked documents or transferred it from one person to another. When I talked to people who went to the property rights offices, there was no shortage of property rights documents just none of it agrees. If you are going to do private sector development, at some point it must be joined [with property rights] and resolved because that is what gets average people the confidence to be able economic actors above the wage labor effort. Nobody has an answer to that. The World Bank doesn't have an answer. USAID doesn't have an answer. It is not a criticism to say we can't do it, because no one else has succeeded either. If we were serious about private sector development, that would be one of the top 2 or 3 things to do. I am not a development expert, so I have always been struck how difficult it is to get any sort of financing going in these places. It is always so owned by an elite or the level of trust necessary to run finance is just not there. Being able to get capital to do economic things is extraordinarily difficult for anyone, but the people who control at the top politically. [Our sanctions against Hawalas] had second order affects. In Accelerating Success, there was a private sector development component and it was focused on building the ring road to get regional trade and transport. There was some agriculture in it. There was a USGS effort that we were going to build some industrial zones. There were probably two or three more things that are escaping my memory, but they were all things that were done other places or were relatively so that you could get something started. **There is always a tension between the grand scheme that opens up a whole domain and building on something that will work, then you can build further on it.** It is the Easterly argument. The grand scheme versus to build on what works. In infrastructure, we had a greater design – we were going to get the ring road built than disperse the ring road. The other places we wanted to just get something going in these domains and then we would get more ambitious over time. **While we were working on Accelerating Success in Washington, there was a consciousness that we will do this, then we need to talk with Afghans and that will be job one when we get to Afghanistan. There was a high degree of consciousness that this was going to be a joint undertaking. In the next phases, everything undertaken was jointly developed because it can only work if you do that.**

Lesson Learned

1. You need standing capabilities for both planning and in each of these domains so that you don't have to create them or have to operate on an ad hoc basis.
2. Funding issue – you have to have operational funding that can be spent on day one and not just by the military but by the civilians.
3. All of this state and nation building, particularly in the security area has to be done with incredible attentiveness to the political consequences of every decision you are making. We often think it is a technocratic act, where it is actually a highly political act when helping to reconstitute a government.
4. There is no perfect or fast solution to problematic actors. Whichever course you take, whether to do deals with them or push them out, you have to ready to deal with the second order

LESSONS LEARNED RECORD OF INTERVIEW

consequences. If you keep them in, you have to police them, if you push them out you have to be prepared to deal with the organized crime they will create. It is like a decision tree. We often stop at the first decision and assume it will be perfect. No you have to manage the second order question.

5. Across the Bush and Obama administrations there seems to be a belief that local political forces, given the opportunity to handle their own politics….just leave them to themselves and it will all be fine. We did well in the Bonn process. We did badly in the CPA. We did horrifically in Libya. The people that have gone through these horrific regimes, whether Saddam or the Taliban, are not going to be ready to seamlessly handle their own politics. They need a supporting handing like the Bonn process or the like. The local equivalent in each case. The probability that it will work out well [absent this support] is low.

6. If you are going to do state building and rebuilding an economy in these kinds of context, it has to be systematic in a way that we have lost. We did some of the best state and nation building the world has ever seen after WWII and in the 50's, so it is not that it can't be done, but you have to be systematic about it and resource it.

7. Like Rumsfeld says, you have to enable them, the local societies to do it. You don't have to do it for them. It doesn't get done by itself.

Follow-Up

1. Embassy Interagency Planning Group
2. Supplemental spending bills
3. Afghan Reach Back Group
4. (b)(3), (b)(6), (b)(7)(C)
5. Khalilzad written statement submitted as part of confirmation hearing
6. October Governance Agreement

LESSONS LEARNED RECORD OF INTERVIEW

Project Title and Code:	
LL-01 – Strategy and Planning	
Interview Title:	
Interview with LTG Michael T. Flynn (Ret.).	
Interview Code:	
LL-01-a14	
Date/Time:	
11/10/2015; 0900-1030	
Location:	
SIGAR HQ, Arlington, VA	
Purpose:	
To elicit interviewee's thoughts on U.S. reconstruction efforts in Afghanistan	
Interviewees: (Either list interviewees below, attach sign-in sheet to this document or hyperlink to a file)	
SIGAR Attendees:	
(b)(6) (b)(6) (b)(6)	
Sourcing Conditions (On the Record/On Background/etc.):	ON THE RECORD
Recorded: Yes	No
Recording File Record Number (if recorded):	
Prepared By: (Name, title and date)	
(b)(6)	
Reviewed By: (Name, title and date)	
Key Topics:	
• Introduction • Information and Access • Violence and the Media • Analysis and Policy • Corruption and Narcotics • Positivity Bias • CIA vs ISAF Intelligence • Mission Statements and Self-Rating • Clarification on Who's Who Analysis	

Introduction

I think that in general, you'll be part of the history of this thing [the war in Afghanistan], obviously because what SIGAR's role has been for a long time. I used to go down and sit with the SIGAR people in Kandahar, just to chat with them, have a cup of coffee, and see what they were up to. Never mind not accomplishing our mission, but the

LESSONS LEARNED RECORD OF INTERVIEW

severity of corruption in our own system, I think is just unbelievable. The waste that I saw is unbelievable. You just sit there and go, "you have got to be kidding me, why did we do this?" I think that somebody, someday, will sit down and do some very serious research with data, which they can discover, [about this problem]. A friend of mine just did an assessment in Iraq. He is a very serious gentleman in this case. He is discovering how little data we actually have kept for [the new military] organization. The Secretary [of Defense] has just appointed our general in Iraq - U.S. Army 3rd Corps. It is amazing. He [my friend conducting the assessment] did a good solid 45 days and went into theater. He has an extraordinary background in the whole theater, but definitely in Iraq. He just told me the other day that it is like we are starting from scratch. In this era of data and information that we have; we have all these things and all this stuff, but everybody goes and then takes [the data] when they leave. You do your right-seat ride and we have actually taken right-seat rides for granted. I am in the process of writing a book right now and part of it is how we have gotten away from that. We are such a strong country, but we have gotten away from the idea of actually how to win anything. **There is a machinery that is behind what we do, and it keeps us participating in the conflict because it generates wealth.** [It generates wealth] all around and on both sides - well all sides...there are more than two sides.

Information and Access

The institution resists that kind of innovation [as I recommended in my report Fixing Intel]. The most innovative time in a human's life is in combat. Your instincts to survive are as turned on as a human being will ever have their instincts turned on. It is as high of a time of instinctual innovation as you can imagine. So does it apply to the big force? I don't know. I still see media on the battlefield today. I just watched a great documentary on these Yazidi women that were taken by ISIS and then tortured and raped. It is unbelievable. Here is this female reporter who is in Syria, who snuck into Syria. We can't do that right now without permission from the President of the United States, but they instead get permission from some producer. They are filming the whole thing: crossing the river, sneaking in, going on boats, and she is driving on the road. Not in any kind of a cover or nothing. It was a blond hair woman. It was unbelievable and the story is amazing. So when I ask the intelligence community where they got the information and they say it is from some INT. I ask what INT and they might say SIGINT. So no one actually talked to anybody? They would say no.

The easiest deception against the U.S. Intelligence Community is SIGINT. The easiest. That is me picking up my phone, knowing that someone is listening to me, and saying "the wedding is on, it will be tomorrow." Of course one of the code words we always listened for and we already thought wedding meant there would be an attack. That was some of the language used for 9/11. That right there, whether anything is going to happen, I just say that and all of a sudden you get an entire country (I have seen this happen) put on alert because of something like that. This happened more than once. In an environment where human behavior is at its most active, which is an insurgency-like effort, where humans interact on the battlefield and not just combat. [You also] are trying to understand a population. Every insurgency that I have studied, and I have studied nearly 30 case studies if not more over the last 10 or 15 years, the population is actually what you are trying to convince. So if you are trying to convince the population, you have to understand the population. That, to me, was sort of one those cold bucket of water over the head moment.

I spent three years hunting human beings to kill them or capture them in Iraq, Afghanistan and East Africa. We refined our processes in Iraq. We experimented with capabilities, techniques and procedures in Iraq. What we learned in Iraq, we began to apply actually globally, because that was JSOC's missions. Our main effort was Iraq, Afghanistan and Somalia, but our mission was global. We did things in other parts of the world including in the Asia-Pacific Theater and in Central and South America. Again during that time, it was against terrorists because that is where they were. So I did that for three years and that was my intelligence mission, it was man hunting. It was capture/kill al-Qaeda and its associated movements and leaders.

LESSONS LEARNED RECORD OF INTERVIEW

All of a sudden I step out of that and I return to a series of assignments, starting with CENTCOM, then the Joint Staff, then back into Afghanistan with ISAF. I then held the Assistant Director for National Intelligence [position], then to DIA. I went back into a world with a very conventional, very structured, very cautious, very archaic intelligence system. [That is of course true beside] the time in Afghanistan where I realized that what we needed to change. So as I was watching things unfold from my perch at CENTCOM, then from my perch at the Joint Staff, particularly inside of the region and inside of Afghanistan, and listening to the failures that we were having, it started to strike me that we were doing a whole range of things incorrect. I am actually looking at the intelligence and I am saying, the intelligence is actually pretty good. The strategic assessments, if you go back and I am not sure if you guys can do this, you may want to go back and look at the NIEs at least, but if you went and looked at strategic intelligence assessments from Central Command, from the last ten years, you would find a stark clarity as to what the intelligence system was assessing in Afghanistan pretty clearly. I think it was very clear. **The policy decisions and the operational decisions, I don't think matched what the intelligence was saying.** I think that there is a biasedness. I am going to draw you a picture here.

First of all, we started the war and then subsequently we continued to focus on the 'where'...where the problem was. Strategically, we focused on where, which is really important because I will get to what we should have started off with and stuck to. So we started on where, because it was, "well where did they [al-Qaeda] come from?" Well they came from Afghanistan, so let's go to Afghanistan. We of course also went to a 'where' called Iraq and why did we go to Iraq? That is the other side, 'why?' So we have got really gotten to this [question of why for Iraq] but we have not gotten to the why [with Afghanistan]. Why did they hate us? Why did they attack us? Why are they operating the way they are operating? Why is the government like this? All the ways you could ask the question 'why' we never really addressed [for Afghanistan]. There has been a bunch of stuff written since 9/11 of course that have tried to address it. There are think tanks and all of these other people. If you pull it all back and dig into some of the great products that have been written. A little bit of Fixing Intel was about the why, in fact, 99% of it was about the why. It was trying to address the why to influence and look backwards as to the where. In between [where and why] then you can have the what and the when. Why did something happen? What did it mean? When do we do something about it and where do we go? The big question in why, first. Why did this happen? Why is it that we have this problem? To me, we have not gotten to this [why]. Politically we are still arguing about why.

I am probably going to make a lousy analogy here. First, the intel system – every component of it wants their intel to be the golden nugget. NGA wants their analysis of their picture so NGA can come in and say "we are the ones that solved the problem, we found [Osama] bin Laden." The SIGINT system wants to come in and say "it was our SIGINT system that found the guy and that is why we were able to get the guy." HUMINT wants to say, "we had the best HUMINT and he led us to the target." **There is an absolute bias in the single INTs** that we have that is why I am a huge believer in the open world of information. That is beyond open source data, it is the open world of information.

I attended a meeting yesterday, because I got back Sunday from Japan. I attended the meeting all day yesterday on cyber and right now there are eight companies that have formed a strategic alliance. They are all U.S.-based companies. They are collecting more in probably five minutes than the intel community is collecting in the same period of time. I can tell you that in a month, and I am guessing and likely underestimating, they are probably collecting five times more than the U.S. Intelligence Community is collecting. This is a commercial alliance. Millions and millions of pieces of information and threat data that they get. Their challenge as a commercial entity is analyzing it. What the intel community has is a gazillion analysts. So you have this inherent bias and this is what we are trying to achieve and everyone is saying "this is mine." That is why the all-source activities we have become very important.

The SOICs are a good example. The SOICs were meant to actually review everything and to validate what it was we were seeing on the battlefield. To the degree that they could, enlightened commanders, particularly enlightened company commanders that saw use them, they would have a much more thorough understanding. A company

LESSONS LEARNED RECORD OF INTERVIEW

commander has an area of operations, so we wanted to gather a level of detail [in there] but the SOICs had the responsibility to bring in the pressure points around the area and bring in the connections. Most people don't know that if you live in Farah province in Afghanistan, if you live in Uruzgan, if you live in Ghazni, or a portion of Paktika, that you are a Kandahari. You are a member of the Kandahari tribe. Now you then can get down into the zai's like the Ghilzais, the Orakzai's, and Noorzais, zai, zai zai. They are all sub-tribes of being a Kandahari. So the end of the day, they are all Kandarharis. If you understand the history of how it unraveled, it is not even six degrees of separation, it is one.

At the beginning of the war (2002-2010), INTs were where we got our intelligence because that was conventionally where we got it and everybody knew it. Facebook didn't come around until 2005 and Twitter was a sound. The information revolution has only occurred in the last 10 years, if you want to stretch it, but really in the last 5 years. The war went on for a long time and INTs were where I was informed. I could also read a really good report out of RAND, CSIS, or CNAS. If I am switched on and really paying attention to open source back then, if I am reading a variety of things, to include history, I could probably know a lot more than the Intelligence Community is going to tell me. The response from policymakers is always "what does the intel say?" **Remember there is an inherent bias in the intel community because they want to get money, they want to exist, and they want to grow.**

Back in 2002, [we only used] 20% of open source [to inform us]. I call this open world information now because if I can see where 1.8 billion people are trending on Twitter that is pretty telling what is important in the world. I can go to my iPhone right now and see what is trending on Twitter for 1.8 billion people and what the mass quantity of those people are thinking. You can see the top 10 trends, just that and never mind other social medium. So the intelligence system and the government system has not broken from this model [of reliance on traditional INTs for a majority of their information]. Again, I call them enlightened commanders or enlightened leaders, will tend to use other things than their intelligence system and I have been a part of it. As a J2 for many years, if my commander knew less than I knew about intelligence, then he was worthless. The best leaders, the best commanders that we have, the best Chairman's, the best Secretaries of Defense, the best Presidents of the United States, if they don't have better intelligence than their heads of intelligence, than they are doing a disservice and they are being irresponsible in the jobs they are serving in.

Violence and the Media

Yes, [people, especially at the NSC level were looking at violence] because it was a very visible thing. That is what sells. That is what the news sells. They sell bad things. Nobody wants to talk about how many schools are being built. Every so often you may get that. Again, I really highlight this idea about leadership. You can get wrapped around the axle about every IED that goes off, but the best counter to an improvised explosive device is security, not another MRAP. Provide security and that will counter the improvised explosive device. Now there are tactics that go with that. I went around Afghanistan and I would sit down with tribal leaders and individuals. I sat down one time and they were describing where we built wells. It was like, why do you guys continue to put these wells in? You are putting them in the wrong places. There were some SOF units that would work with their counterparts and would actually figure out where to put them in. To say that an Afghan can't dig a hole or know where to put a well is amazing. They know where their wells are and where the water is at, yet we have engineers saying we have to put a well here. [We would place wells] between two tribes to try and bring the tribes together. Insane. Totally insane. It is not a model that works for them.

[Early on] we would rely a little on this [open source] and a lot on the INTs. You may have an individual like Eric Schmidt, who has a great article out today, and people will say that he does not know what he is saying. But some of these reporters have far more combat experience and actually go talk to these individuals because they are able to get into villages. They [Afghans] know that they are media. There is a trust, almost like if you are from the military I [Afghans] can't trust you.

LESSONS LEARNED RECORD OF INTERVIEW

What has changed and had an impact on the U.S. Intelligence Community is that it is now 90% of open source or open world of information [that they use]. There is now a richness now that comes in this final 10% [of the traditional INTs]. We might have Hamid Karzai's phone tapped, ▓▓▓▓▓▓▓ (b)(3) ▓▓▓▓▓▓▓

Those are very finite pieces of information. They are typically very strategic – this 10%. Sometimes their latency makes it more irrelevant for timeliness. Sometimes, it can be very relevant. It can be a piece of SIGINT. [For example] it seems like the U.S. got some SIGINT when this Russian plane was blown up in the sky. It sounds to me like it was just somebody in the Sinai talking to somebody in Syria and it was picked up. So if we picked it up in SIGINT and it was two of these individuals talking to each other and they are boasting about it, I hope that at some channel that we actually told President [Abdel Fattah] el-Sisi and President Putin that we picked it up. Why hide that? Tell the world that we collected signal intelligence of these guys talking. Do you know how many they change phones? Just find them again. So there is a relevancy still to this [traditional INTs] but it is strategic and policymakers still tend to want this [traditional INTs] and not this [open source]. I don't think they know what to do with [open source information] and it is [to them], what is the reliability? I actually think that it is in the analysis and instincts and the experience is where the reliability comes in.

Analysis and Policy

I don't need much information at all to trust my instincts and my experience when it comes to certain things. I don't need somebody to take me through an hour briefing. What is the subject? What is it you are going to ask me to do? Let's have a conversation because [they] can trust that I inform myself properly during the course of my daily activities and I have enough experience on that issue. What I want to do is give my experience back. So I trust the analyst. I get to know somebody and I ask how long they have been doing this and they might say twenty five years. I may ask if they focused on Afghanistan and Pakistan and if they say yes, that is all I need to know to know. Then I can have a conversation with somebody and trust that they know what they are talking about. That might be an intel person or intel analyst, but do they have the expertise on operations and policy? Maybe not. Have they talked to commanders and policymakers? Sure. **I think that policymakers, the ones I have gotten to know, and there have been plenty of them, only touch the subject episodically, instead of living it and breathing it for a lifetime.** You are going to get some policymakers [who say otherwise]. If you are a policymaker you are being driven by a political leader who is politically appointed and goes in and out of government. [This person] may go to a think tank or go do something on their own in business, but it is political. They live and breathe on the political scheme. **As for the professional policymakers that are in the bureaucracy, I am not so sure how much their voice is heard and how much they are able to actually push an agenda that should be consistent over time despite the political agenda.**

Corruption and Narcotics

We did the raid on the New Ansari Bank. It was huge. I thought it was a huge success. We conducted that raid and in three days, we did a lot of exploitation. We brought in like 45 people from around the country very quietly [to help with the exploitation]. We parked them inside of ISAF headquarters and I even brought McChrystal over to thank the people we dragged in. We did it in coordination with the Minister of Interior, [Mohammad Hanif] Atmar, who at the time was incredibly courageous to do it. We literally went there and surrounded the bank and had a standoff. We took all of the data. We did it on a Thursday night to have the thing back up and operational by Saturday night/Sunday. We used Friday for their kind of holiday period to exploit as much as we could. **The lead up to that was that the New Ansari was just incredibly corrupt. It had double books and people were just stealing us blind.** Money was being siphoned through it – hundreds of thousands of dollars, millions probably. The Central Bank of Kabul was involved.

The U.S. Embassy was involved to a degree. **The overall outcome...was anyone held accountable? No, no one was held accountable.** There should be data on that. One of the guys that did that is out now but is a good friend.

LESSONS LEARNED RECORD OF INTERVIEW

His name was 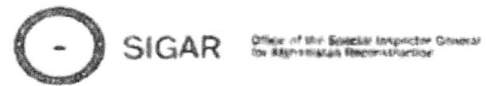 he was DEA. He just changed jobs but he did the DEA Major Crimes Task Force. That was actually the beginning of the Anti-Corruption Task Force. McMasters comes in with Petraeus, but really we had the Anti-Corruption Task Force going on for a while. Andrea Thompson is another one, she is still in. Colonel Thompson came and worked for me. She became sort of a quasi-lead for me. She is in town here and works Congressman McCaul.

I also saw intelligence, and we knew it, that Hawala system that was run by the Taliban out of Kandahar. I mean they had one Hawala and that was part of the whole New Ansari system. They had like one Hawala in Kandahar in 2000. Then in 2009 they were in 29 countries. It is actually moving money, narcotics money, probably our [U.S. money], was being moved globally. I believe, and I think I saw enough evidence, where the Central Bank of Kabul was adjusting their rates to the U.S. dollar off of a Hawala. So the money that was in, they could adjust it. It was the whole thing about buying currency. You sell high, buy low. Money that needed to be moved through contracting and through narcotics.

The narcotics today, is the worst it has ever been. I don't think that there was a year that has gone by in our time in Afghanistan where the narcotics industry has had a bad year. I think it has been progressively, on a scale, progressively moved up. There was a lot of things we did we tried to do to reduce that, but narcotics was not a big mission for the international force. [However], it was driving a lot of the funding for the enemy that we were facing.

Yes, [confronting this would have meant confronting Fahim and Bismuilah Khan]. I was in his office [Fahim's] and it was not pretty [when we confronted some of his Air Force generals]. You know what, arrest the guy. This is a combat zone. Arrest him. If they want to fight us, fine. Fight us, but arrest them. They should have arrested every one of them and thrown them all in jail. I will tell you that all of the threats that came out of that, from those that I remember, I thought that we should have arrested them. Yes, [in the Air Force case and the shooting], they should have been arrested and brought up on charges by us. Not by the international assistance force and not under some lousy Afghan court. **There are a lot of guys that should have been arrested. You have to have accountability. That is part of the problem with instilling confidence in a population – they see it [corruption] happening right in front of their eyes. We see it happening and we don't look the other way, we actually enable it.**

I will give you a good story of probably one of the wealthiest people in Afghanistan today. He started out as a young interpreter in the very early days. He owns a couple of banks. He owns a rental SUV service. He rents interpreters. He is a young guy and savvy as Afghans are. He is an interpreter and a not very good one. He literally was like 21 or 22 and was doing interpretation for a commander and this was day with no problem with bags of money (b)(3) ▓▓▓▓▓▓▓▓▓▓▓▓▓▓▓▓▓▓▓▓▓▓▓▓▓▓▓▓ Talk about lack of accountability. So this commander is using this interpreter and the commander says I need 'this' to this Afghan guy he is talking to. The commander says that he will buy 'it' from you. The man [who is selling the item] says he will sell the item for a couple of hundred dollars. The interpreter then says [to the commander] $20,000. The commander says, okay, no problem. The interpreter gives the man a few hundred dollars and the takes the rest of it because he is a savvy businessman. He keeps doing that and keeps doing it and doing it. The money is more and more and he is cutting deals. Everybody loves this interpreter. Everybody thinks the world of him. He drives around in a big up-armored SUV inside of Kabul today. He has security all over him and if you want to rent a nice, clean SUV, black, and everybody does, you will rent it from his company. He also owns a couple of banks. That is a real story and a real person. He is all of 34 of 35 [years old] as of today. How many others of him are there? There are probably hundreds of those types of individuals who benefited because, frankly, we didn't know what we were doing.

When I got to Afghanistan in the summer of 2009, one of the things that we had talked to the Chairman about, prior to going and prior to the big decision to replace McKiernan with McChrystal, we talked about the Af-Pak hands program. That was in winter or spring of 2009. We wanted to build this Af-Pak hands program and when the decision was made to change it, there was this big push. So when we get to Afghanistan, there is only one officer on

LESSONS LEARNED RECORD OF INTERVIEW

the ISAF staff that could speak Dari. That was an Air Force Brigadier General. He was there in the summer of 2009. He self-taught himself. He was in the CSTC-A staff I think. He was a good guy and I met him, but he was only their briefly. The Air Force pulled him out in like July and sent him to Japan. So here is a guy who we could have used, and we laughed about it because this is how insane this [system] is. I always use the example that in WWII where we trained like 2,000 [people] in a tier 3 language called Japanese to support the war effort. Not interpreters, but actual members of the military. We could not even train five in Dari. The intel community did some SIGINT people but I know of others that did some self-training, but it is ridiculous. Even today, we are still in Afghanistan and you go tell me how many actual U.S. members of the military or policy [community], or from State who speak Dari or Pashto. That is a shame and that is a policy decision.

The intelligence system, I thought was very accurate on the who is who in the zoo there, so to speak. Who is who in the leadership of those who we were facing in Afghanistan and also the members of the international coalition. **The international coalition was also corrupt and also saw the U.S. money coming in and took advantage of it. Don't think it was just the Afghans. There was a lot of intel about other countries and people that were there taking advantage of deals, including us. That is why I say that there is probably criminal cases waiting to be had against people who found weaknesses in our system. Even soldiers and other government officials found weaknesses in our system to make money.** The tactical intelligence and the reporting that was captured in terms of written down and databased in some computer system that described corruption, was unbelievable. There was plenty of it.

Positivity Bias

As intelligence makes its way up higher, it gets consolidated and really watered down; it gets politicized. It gets politicked because once policymakers get their hands on it, and frankly once operational commanders get their hands on it, they put their twist to it. My news before 9 o'clock in the morning was never good. If I brought good news in, it was that we captured or killed somebody, we just found out something, we just did something that actually worked out okay that was an intelligence success, or we found somebody. For a while it might have made me feel good, but after 2006, for me, it was actually irrelevant because we were just killing so many people and it wasn't making any difference at all. We were capturing a lot of people too. Commanders and policymakers, on the spectrum of news, they want to always be good news. **Operational commanders, State Department policymakers, and Department of Defense policymakers are going to be inherently rosy in their assessments. They will be unaccepting of hard hitting intelligence.**

CIA vs ISAF Intelligence

(b)(1), (b)(3)

What I learned was that the CIA was not sharing all of their information with the Department of Defense or the rest of the Intelligence Community for that matter. I asked why and [they said] it was operational traffic. So the CIA has operational cables that don't make it into intelligence reporting, which is absolutely irresponsible. They are an intelligence agency so their operational traffic and their intelligence traffic, to me, is intelligence. I don't need, in their operational traffic, their sourcing. I need the richness of the report. (b)(1), (b)(3) What I saw was the incredibly ineffective reporting system that the CIA has. I hands-on saw it. I know what their system is. They were not providing intelligence from operational reports to the rest of the Intelligence Community.

So now you have this disconnect and I wanted to know about that disconnect, (b)(1), (b)(3) and when I asked why they couldn't share they said it was operational traffic, not intel. So wait a second, you [CIA] are an intel agency. **This is where the intelligence leadership is irresponsible for not**

LESSONS LEARNED RECORD OF INTERVIEW

sharing intelligence in and among themselves. Back to the alliance I told you about that has better intelligence than the intelligence community because everything is intelligence to them.

[redacted (b)(1), (b)(3)] We would come up with the 83 Districts for our Campaign Plan and we used that [redacted (b)(1), (b)(3)] I think 83 was the number and we might have added one additional district, General Rodriguez may have added on later on and it may have been around Kabul.

[redacted (b)(1), (b)(3)] **Operationally the reporting that comes out of there [ISAF] is wonderful; it is rosy.** So I am on VTC with the Secretary of Defense, CENTCOM Commander, ISAF Commander (with McChrystal and Petraeus), and I give my presentation and it sucks. It is almost like disregarded but it is "okay, got it. Here is what we are going to do, strategically."

Mission Statements and Self-Rating

To me this is a really important point. If you go back and look at the mission statements for every battalion and every brigade from the beginning of the war, they are essentially all the same. It is "defeat and destroy the enemy and protect the population." [This was true for every] battalion commander and every brigade commander from a U.S.-side. It is essentially those same two things – defeat the enemy and protect the population. So they all went in for whatever their rotation was, 9 months or 6 months, and were given that mission, accepted that mission and executed that mission. **Then they all said, when they left, they accomplished that mission. Every single commander.** Not one commander is going to leave Afghanistan, or Iraq or any place, not one is going to leave and say, "you know what, we didn't accomplish our mission." So the next guy that shows up finds it [their area] screwed up, after a great right-seat ride. They do their mission analysis once they are on the ground and then they come back and go "man this is really bad," but the last battalion, regiment or BCT, accomplished their mission. They have all of these wonderful stats about what they did. I am telling you that this is true from 2002 until today.

From ambassadors down to the low level, [they all say] we are doing a great job. Really? So if we are doing such a great job, why does it feel like we are losing? I was supposed to testify this Thursday in front of the Senate Homeland Security Committee, Chairman Johnson's committee, but they moved it. I am going to walk through my testimony. My testimony is on ISIS in the Middle East and the threat to the Homeland. I have been working on my testimony for about a week and doing a lot of research. Every measurable activity is failing. So when you look at Afghanistan, every single measurable activity is failing. If [General] John Campbell were to sit here today and say [that is not true because,] we have built more schools, we have more cars on the road...really? Afghanistan is better today than it was? There are more people, I guess, in the city of Kabul. The reports right now in Helmand province is that the Taliban have completely retaken Marjah and are about to retake Lashkar Gah. So you know, really? We have done better? So every single operational commander, battalion commander, regimental, BCT, RC – every single one came in [to Afghanistan] and said the situation was not like they thought it and when they left that they had defeated the enemy; we have convinced the population and helped the population. [They all said] that they gave it over [to the next commander] and I said, here it is, it is in great shape and they love us down here. Then you come in and you say, ok, I am here and I have a year. My first 30 days, [I think] this is really bad, but I guarantee you that if you look at the out-briefs you will see nothing but goodness. Believe me, I was looking at them for 10 years. I saw this in Iraq and really dug into it in Afghanistan.

I will give you one other picture. I saw this in Iraq and did a little bit of research in Afghanistan. This is in general, but this study was done by General Casey in 2006 for Iraq. For Afghanistan, I did my own sort of [review] that was anecdotal. I thought it was pretty thorough. It was looking at mission statements and end of mission results. A unit comes in [to country] and comes in at a certain level or tempo. They are going to be there for 12 months. So when I

LESSONS LEARNED RECORD OF INTERVIEW

[a unit commander] comes in, it takes about three months to find an operational rhythm. I [as commander have new guys, not everyone came for the right-seat ride. Some of our battalions are bringing in new recruits the day they are getting ready to deploy in some cases. That is how bad our personnel system was. So I get to a rhythm and then I operate to about the 9 month mark. I have a high operational rate [for those 6 months] and then all of a sudden I begin to drop off until I depart. I [would ask] why is that?

The other part of this is when you look at casualty rates. When do casualties occur? They occurred here [during the three month ramp up] and here [during the three month ramp down]. There is a lack of readiness [in the first three months] and there is complacency [in the final three months] because [the unit] is looking to get out of there. The operational tempo [at the end] is just way down, including the number of patrols and out of sector missions. So you lost some guys here [in the beginning] and had casualties along the timeline. To me this is the Vietnam affect. So if you really study this, you would find a trend. You would find a very clear trend of casualty rates, op-tempo and you could really measure whether or not we were successful. Intelligence has nothing to do with this. At the end, when I leave, everybody gets a high-five. You can kind of tell the great leaders and the great units [because] they will have less casualties and less wounded because of the way they operate. The best units, they come in at a higher level, get to a higher level [of operational tempo] quicker, perform for a longer period of time, and tend to not let up [as early]. These are your Special Forces and select units out of places like the 82nd or some from the 101st. I am not talking about battalions, I am talking about regiments and companies.

This sense that we are doing great, permeates all the way up to the top. As a senior intel officer for many years, my assessments were not good. Things [I wrote said] said it was not at all going well. Never. We are basically fighting the wrong way. **We are participating in conflict, we are not really here to win. There is corruption in reporting and not just corruption in the theft that occurred.** This was irresponsible, to be kind, in reporting operationally that everything was wonderful. That also includes from the State Department. There is no way that over the years, to include this year, that we can say things are wonderful. All of the indexes that judge the country of Afghanistan are all still down in the bottom. The attack on this training camp, the number in there was 160 in the camp, never mind around the country. So when we would say, hey we have a problem with al-Qaeda and a problem with LeT (and I am talking about LeT in Kandahar and not up in the eastern province), and we are talking about this group called the Khorasan group for years. We would say we don't see al-Qaeda as a threat at the higher level. Wait a second, here is the reporting, here is the intelligence.

You guys should ask for the ▓(b)(3)▓ assessments ▓(b)(3)▓. You should see if you can get copies ▓(b)(3)▓ They are very sensitive. Typically, they are supposed to be read by the President of the United States, especially for combat zones. I have read probably 5 or 6 years worth of them and ▓(b)(3)▓ **I can tell you that there is not one** ▓(b)(3)▓ **that I read that would say anything is going in the right direction.** So when it [the negative assessment] gets to the Director of the CIA or the Director of National Intelligence, what happens? Is it [just considered] one ▓(b)(3)▓ opinion? ▓(b)(3)▓

You should see if you can pull them back from 2006 or 2007 maybe, for at least Afghanistan. I think it would be a very interesting read. They are usually pretty short reads and you could get through one in an hour. **I can't remember one that gave a rosy picture, not one. So how do we come to grips with what the intelligence community says and what the operational and policy community is saying? I would tell you, there is huge, huge political biasedness in this. The reason is that there is a political bias and the reason is that there is lack of courage in senior government officials to tell the truth. That is civilian and in the military.** Political and government.

LESSONS LEARNED RECORD OF INTERVIEW

Clarification on Who's Who Analysis

I would not say those reports were from 2002 onward, but maybe pieces of it. I can tell you it was definitely 2008. When I was in CENTCOM, we were doing quite a bit of it. [They] are assessments of the key players, leadership assessments of Afghans, the Afghan Ministers, and the Coalition leadership that we had in the Coalition. These are all U.S. things. We wanted to do assessments of the next RC capital commander. You know, who is this guy? Same with the Germans. With all of these guys, it is like, who are we dealing with? Then we had our own little HUMINT network to look at if these guys are talking with the enemy.

# Lessons Learned Record of Interview

Project Title	
LLP01 – Strategy and Planning	
Interview Code:	
LL-01 (b)(3), (b)(6)	
Date/Time:	
August 25, 2015 / 14:30 – 15:30	
Location:	
Washington, DC	
SIGAR Attendees:	
Candace Rondeaux, Matthew Sternenberger	

Non- attribution Basis:	Yes	x	No		
Recorded:	Yes		No	x	

Recording File Record Number:

Prepared By: (Name, title and date)
Matthew Sternenberger, Research Analyst, 8/26/2015

Reviewed By: (Name, title and date)

Key Topics:
- Afghanistan overview
- Observations and Examples with Oversight Mechanisms
- Necessary Introspection
- PRTs and Logistics
- Current Critiques of Strategy and SIGAR
- International Perspective
- Lessons

Afghanistan Overview

(b)(3), (b)(6), (b)(7)(C), (b)(7)(D)

Most Americans hold the view that the strategy in Afghanistan has not succeeded and the rest believe that there are many other places much more dangerous than Afghanistan; it is an uphill battle to the U.S. Overall, it seems that security assistance is less vulnerable and slower to temper – likely because it is structured differently and now under Overseas Contingency Operations.

Observations and Examples with Oversight Mechanisms

What surprises me is that you are talking to National Security Council (NSC) people and not with people from the U.S. Agency for International Development (USAID). The NSC is supposed to track implementation ensure that resources are going toward the intended objectives. While we are tasked to track this

SIGAR-LL-01-00124

implementation, we must get our information from the relevant agencies. There is no independent stream of information and our job is to hold them accountable. It is obvious that there is a disconnect between the strength of our core investments and our desired affects. We must give people a discount that has not been afforded to them. For example, we question USAID on a program they are implementing, but should we even be doing that program in the first place? There is a bigger question here – why does the U.S. undertake actions that are beyond its abilities? This question gets at strategy and human psychology, and it is a hard question to answer. It [Afghanistan] is not government-in-a-box or nation-building. The military is equally as guilty too of biting off more than they can chew. Development is more criticized, in part, due to the SIGAR mandate but the Department of Defense (DOD) Operations and Maintenance (O&M) costs are not under equal scrutiny. USAID is over-scrutinized.

USAID and the DOD have different barriers to scrutiny. While it is true there is a lot of scrutiny, it is grossly insufficient regarding the DOD O&M and conflict. We just don't question the DOD in the same way as we question development agencies in conflict zones. "**We don't scrutinize DOD fuel costs because we have institutionalized it and adopted a "that's how it goes" notion.**" We have formalized $100 per gallon as normal for the DOD. This is potentially a bad way of warfighting.

There have been some people in the Pentagon who are looking at this, but they have been doing it is private or semi-private. If we look at the Mine-Resistant Ambush Protected (MRAP) program [vehicle]. We had a surge of MRAPs into Afghanistan to protect against $300 improvised explosive devices (IEDs). Now we have cut those [MRAPs] into razor blades. Is this just the cost of doing business? The full burden of the MRAP program seems to be just how we do business and not in support of the military or even in support of COIN.

When we look at COIN as economic assistance (digging wells or building school) and not as military tool, it looks like our spending was wasteful and ugly. One of [General] McChrystal's hardest lessons was his government-in-a-box program which typified the American wartime machinery and he thought you could simply wave a magic wand and POOF!

Necessary Introspection

Why did it get to this point? The answer is much broader than SIGAR and is about human psychology and national security policy making – the complexities will take a long time to unravel. Our entire post-9/11 response is all subject to question because of this increasing complexity. Why did we make the Taliban the enemy when we were attacked by Al Qaeda? Why did we want to defeat the Taliban? Why did we think it was necessary to build a hyper-function state to forgo the return of the Taliban? In fairness the people I know in government believed we were guilt of nation-building.

If the civilians are not doing their part, on rule of law or governance for example, is all this for not? Should we even do it? If this [rule of law and governance] is what the military needs, then the military may be forced to do it or contract it out.

"**Ashraf Ghani was the original SIGAR.**" Ghani [then Minister of Finance] said, early on, that the methodology the U.S. had for building roads in Afghanistan was flawed and will have unintended consequences. USAID and State, said that we can't do it Ghani's way because we are not structurally equipped to do so. Ghani said that the U.S. should just give the money to the Afghans and they will build the roads and will likely do it at 1/10th of the cost but that is just not how we do economic assistance. We are not comfortable just writing a check and saying, go forth, do it.

Provincial Reconstruction Teams (PRT) and Logistics

PRTs would have been on Ghani's hit list. "**Administering aid through PRTs made sense on one level to synchronize efforts between the embassy and ISAF. It sounds good and works on PowerPoint.**" It was really about coordination of strategy, a whole of government approach and wanting control.

Lessons Learned Record of Interview

"We have institutionalized the dysfunction because we want control of a synchronized strategy."

The MRAP is a prime example of this and so is the fuel distribution process – we transport fuel with helicopters to the provinces! Soldiers get pizza and ice cream while out in the provinces instead of getting food from local vendors. This is all happening because that is just the nature of the military logistical system.

Current Critiques of Strategy and SIGAR

Isaiah Wilson has written on the point that COIN has failed in the modern era. COIN forces today are disconnected from their area of operation and resupply is thousands of miles away. Instead of seeking security from the community, they hide in MRAPs; instead of sourcing food locally, they have it imported. *"The modern COIN forces are like aliens parachuting in and staying only for short rotations with no sense of the landscape."*

Economic development efforts have not been just wasteful but have been institutionalized within COIN in unique ways which need to be re-examined. Really, both the military and the civilian side need to have their structures re-examined. [Ambassador] Eikenberry also wrote a good critique, despite it being a bit personal, which hit many of these same themes.

It is understandable that it has been hard get at the ineffective or dysfunctional narrative. The hard question is how does this dysfunction happen? Most will eventually conclude that we should not have implemented the strategy that we did. There is a lot of noise over this disagreement because of SIGAR and how what SIGAR says is often seen as cheap shots at agencies just wasting money. But in the conflict zone and in the bureaucracy that is within, there is a larger infection and structural dysfunction. People are quite defensive because there often is no context [to SIGAR's reports] and the reports are seen in an accusatory way.

People have said and continue to say that Afghanistan has improved despite all of these mistakes. When authors are making this claim they run through a long list of metrics about mortality, education, nutrition etc.

I would argue that it is all similarly and structurally handicapped. Like how COIN is grossly ineffective because of the complicated environments. That said, it is less a target since the inefficiencies in the DOD O&M far exceed civilian agencies waste during peak war. For example, there is $120 billion for DOD O&M, $12 billion for security assistance and $2.5 billion for civil development. The focus seems to be on the $12 billion or the $2.5 billion and never on the $120 billion for the DOD. The DOD is not just a job program for the U.S. Army and the affects may be more adverse than most know (care for wounded, costs of PTSD etc), but this critique is missing.

Overall it was our assumption that security would improve from 2008 to 2012 as we increased resources and that we would see a return on our investment. Generals Petraeus and Allen had faith that what happened in Iraq would happen in Afghanistan, but that never materialized. In terms of the big picture, there were many questions that were not uncovered because there was no reason to look at certain issues and also SIGAR came into being. *"We were just moving too fast, with too many people and too many resources."* The big picture question is also about what are we doing here [in Afghanistan]? What did we get for this $1 trillion effort? Was it worth $1 trillion? These conversations are only happening in private.

After the killing of Osama Bin Laden, I said that Osama was probably laughing in his watery grave considering how much we have spent on Afghanistan. Tom Donnelly always was asking for cost comparisons to other programs [both domestic and international].

Collectively the system is incapable of taking a step back to question basic assumptions. Again, I point to human psychology as to why this is difficult. [This resistance to introspection] is hard wired in us and part of our evolution.

Lessons Learned Record of Interview

International Perspective

Most people, even in Europe offer criticism and those we should take seriously but still they believe that some response [to the attacks on 9/11] was warranted. They also say that the U.S. response exceeded what was necessary. This includes the over-aggregation of the enemy to include the Taliban as part of our response to al Qaeda. Why, if we were focused on al Qaeda, were we talking about the Taliban? Why were we talking about the Taliban all the time instead of focusing our strategy on al Qaeda?

Micah Zenko recently wrote about the myth of terrorist safe havens and this question about why al Qaeda was connected to the Taliban through this safe haven defense. **Chris Fair** also just published an article about how Pakistan is really the big problem and that it is time we take the kids gloves off.

We have tied ourselves in a Gordian knot. The knot is that while the C. Fair article makes sense, it was not true for most of the period as we did have an al Qaeda-focused strategy and we had to get in bed with and acknowledge that Pakistan was a state sponsor of terrorism, but the Taliban was not as high on the list of priorities for us. We had to work with Pakistan to get to al Qaeda despite Pakistan helping the Taliban. Al Qaeda was a higher strategic objective. Maybe C. Fair's argument is better received now, but that was not always true; we can't sacrifice our top priority.

Lessons

1. Choose your enemies wisely. I recently wrote a piece on this for Foreign Policy (they changed the title however).
2. Don't over-aggregate the enemy.
3. Militarizing a response to criminal attack will lead to a host of problems (terrorism is a criminal act, not an act of war).
4. The process for monitoring and implementing strategy lacks introspection. There is too much momentum and not enough reflection.
5. Staying the course is a costly fallacy.
6. National pride and politics matter as they did in the 2003 invasion and the 2008 [U.S.] elections – both contributed to the problem. Obama simplified the narrative into a good war (Afghanistan) versus bad war (Iraq) theme. It was a useful narrative for the 2008 elections and then it all fell apart and became a liability.

Lessons Learned Record of Interview

Project Title:	
LL-05	
Interview Code:	
LL-05-c15	
Date/Time:	
2/25/2016	
Location:	
Washington, DC (over the phone)	
Purpose:	
To discuss GEN Brian Copes (Ret.) experience in Afghanistan as Joint Chief of Staff of the Army National Guard and the Air National Guard	
Interviewees:	
GEN (Ret.) Brian Copes	
SIGAR Attendees:	
Margaret Jacobson, Research Analyst	
Non-attribution Basis: Yes / No x	On the record, check back for direct quotes
Recorded: Yes / No x	
Recording File Record Number: N/A	
Prepared By: (Name, title and date)	
Margaret Jacobson, Research Analyst 2/3/2016	
Reviewed By: (Name, title and date)	
Paul Fishstein, Team Lead, March 6, 2016	
Key Topics:	

- Civil Affairs
- Whole of Government Approach
- USAID
- ADT vs. DoS mentality
- My Criteria for Projects
- More Money Doesn't Mean Better
- COIN
- Abandoning Development
- Bottom-up Development is Better than Top-Down
- Model for Inter-Agency Development
- Effects of 2014 drawdown
- Divergence in viewpoints between Civilian Affairs and conventional military

Key takeaways:

Lessons Learned Record of Interview

- Whole of Government approach works best when each senior agency official treats each other as equals
- USAID is not designed to create a self-sustaining Afghanistan
- Money starts with Congress, we should not have been given so much money
- ADT thought small and impactful vs. DoS thought large with greater $ amounts
- Projects should be small, impactful and affordable to the Afghan
- Bottom-up development from the grassroots is better than the top-down approach we implemented
- PRTs and ADTs should fall under DoS
- Effects of the military drawdown on ongoing activities

My first comment is don't confuse activity with achievement or accomplishment. A predictable road to failure is to look at high numbers which only measure input not impact. I was on PRT Khowst on FOB Chapman.

Civil Affairs: Civil Affairs soldiers and CAT (Civil Affairs Teams) were farmed out to various combat outposts. The CA soldier is one of the most mature and capable soldiers that had a great sophisticated view of the world. The E-5s (SGT) and E-6s (SSG) were far beyond any MAJ and LTC on the kinetic side of the Army. The kinetic side had no soft skills. That was the strength of the reserve component. They weren't active duty soldiers and only knew how to do Army things. Security was the 800 pound gorilla, but it was about the hearts and minds and altering the Afghan culture.

The crack cocaine of development was how much money was spent. It was an addiction that affected every agency.

Whole of Government Approach: I was blessed to have an O-6 (COL) that really understood the whole of government approach (b)(6) He shaped how the military interacted with the civilians and created a board of directors. With the whole of government approach- there was one rep from State and USDA, and the Army Corps of Engineers. (b)(6) always told his civilian counterpart that "you are my equal" I'm the senior DOD official and you are the senior rep of your department, so we will make decisions together.

USAID: USAID in my opinion is a government agency that has lost its way. The agency's mission is to perpetually involve itself in projects to justify its existence (meaning locals are dependent on USAID so USAID can continue to exist, USAID doesn't work itself out of job so the locals can be independent). USAID built national level contracts and contractors would go out and allegedly do what USAID wants- and send pics of the projects. We (the ADTs) went and found only 4 of the 14 projects. There was no QA/QC (Quality Assurance/ Quality Control) on USAID's part. No one could go into the field. It was in part because the environment was not permissive and prohibited normal procedures for conducting QA/QC. As a result contractors cut corners to maximize profit. The contractors had to pay off HIG (Hezb-e Islami Gulbuddin) or the mob to not disrupt the project. That is why there was shoddy work and construction because money went to HIG vs. quality materials.

Of the three PRT commanders I found one to be a "B" and the other two to be "Cs." The Navy and Air Force did not send their best and brightest- the ones that would go on to future senior level positions. The PRT was Frankenstein- with a whole bunch of parts from DOD put together to make a whole. This presented a leadership challenge. The commanders were not equipped to lead in a

Lessons Learned Record of Interview

complex environment- and were not postured for success. This was out of their league. PRTs were an afterthought.

Money Starts With Congress: How much money was spent starts with Congress. Congress gives us money to spend and expects us to spend all of it. No one in the military is going to go back and say we really don't need all this money, we only need X amount of money. The attitude became we don't care what you do with the money as long as you spend it. That was wrong.

I've never heard of TFBSO. Maybe under another name, but not TFBSO.

ADT vs. DoS mentality: When I went to Afghanistan, I expected to be frustrated by the Afghans, but I was not prepared to be frustrated by our US agencies. We equipped the Ag extensions so the Afghan government could train the farmers- so they can have face to face and see what their government is doing for them. We didn't train the Afghans, we had the government train the Afghans. We coordinated with the Department of State. Except the Department of State didn't like what we were doing, it said we were thinking too small and we needed to develop a juice factory. This idea came from a career developer from the Department of State or USAID who did development in Ukraine and through it was a good idea for Afghanistan.

My Criteria for Projects: I have three guiding principles for doing a project. Ideas identified that could help develop solutions had to meet 3 criteria, which worked in Khowst Province and I have no doubt will work in other areas like Parwan.

1) Had to be reproducible using locally available supplies and materials
2) Had to be affordable for the average farmer who is making a buck a day. Ex: making a greenhouse out of rebar that is in the $100-300 range
3) It has to be sustainable in knowledge and materials including spare parts- that will last for generations

So the solution doesn't make the criteria focused on short term results.

More Money Doesn't Mean Better: There was a $30,000 greenhouse and the bottom was composed of various materials not sustainable by the local Afghan. We had a team member make a greenhouse for $55 that did exactly what the $30,000 greenhouse did. It started the growing season sooner- now I can convince an Afghan to spend $55 on a greenhouse because it works and it's cheap.

(b)(6) showed me a map of Khowst and where all the roads were constructed. He leans over and tells me- How this is all decided- it's all corrupt. All the sub governors asked for a road and their contractors benefited from it. I said how is that any different from the US? Corporate companies benefit from the government. It doesn't matter what the culture is- business is business- people are people. The Afghans are motivated by the same things Americans are.

COIN: The agriculture mission was not a humanitarian one. It was COIN – separating the population from the insurgents. If it was humanitarian, we wouldn't care where we went, we would just help people. There was a reason why we went to some villages and not others. Some districts had 15% of the province's population vs. .2% in another district. We went to the districts with the greater population to get more bang for your buck. The road-trade corridor did allow for farmers to get goods to market. It did have an economic benefit. We would spend time on both sides of the road to positively influence the populace.

Lessons Learned Record of Interview

Abandoning Development: By 2011 we started shaving the security platoon for the AG teams and we were told to use the PRT security, which would drastically reduce our missions because the PRT commander had other priorities. By 2012- a year later, security was taken away from the PRT. Governance, Rule of Law fell by the wayside and we had to compete for scraps. Security became #1. Senior military had abandoned the governance, economic and rule of law effort.

The planned drawdown of 2014 precipitated this. Security retained its prominence. There was a slight rebalancing away from security, but the focus was now on Bagram and Kabul at the Ministry Level. It's just senior officials working at the national level. The most effort is in the north and west, and the south in Kandahar- less so in the east.

Bottom-up Development is better than Top-down: The top-down strategy was a flawed strategy from the beginning. I don't want criticize the people who made these decisions, because I think they did the best they could under the circumstances. But we have to realize that our country didn't start from the top down. We grudgingly created a federal government [The US created its own federal government in 1776]. So why did we think we could have created a central government given the decentralized nature of Afghanistan? We should have modeled the approach after the 13 colonies. However, we don't have the political will. That would take a 10-20 year effort.

We need to focus on low dollar-high impact. It's not about the money, it's about small projects on the local level. Thousands of small projects on the ground would have been better than these large dollar projects.

CERP was the monetary vehicle that was available for people to use. The funding stream for development has to emanate from DoS not DOD. He who holds the purse strings holds the power. However, the DoS resource is not equipped to operate on the level the military can, on the ground. – Career Foreign Service officers are not experienced and equipped to operate in Afghanistan. Early in the conflict DOD should be in charge, but should then dip down and transition to DoS. It was an uncomfortable balance who was in charge. It was never clear that DoS was in charge.

The Integrated Civ-Mil Campaign plan written in 2009 that was co-signed by Eikenberry and McChrystal was a good document to articulate the roles of each agency. It just was not executed well. We are winding down now, so there is no political will to follow through.

Model for Inter-Agency Development: A good model is the civ-mil memo of agreement I had the Ag person, PRT commander, Maneuver element, DoS and USAID sign. It outlined guiding principles and goals to achieve. This was based on assets. It was a simple unifying agreement that was people centric, not project centric. We complemented each other not conflicted with each other.

It's a wrestling match on who should control the PRTs and ADTs- they are going to fall under the military, but should have been under DoS. I think we are smart enough to construct a way to have the PRT and ADT assets fall under DoS and make it work. I'm going to be critical of the Active Duty military, because they breed a certain culture. They keep choosing people that act and look like them. You can take a 3 or 4 star general who can provide operational and logistical guidance, but they shouldn't tell the PRTs and ADTs what to do. They should answer to DoS. The PRTs and ADTs should have been guided by state- that's why the lines of effort were conflicted. However, you would be hard pressed to find a military commander willing to relinquish control.

[We ran out of time before we could get into PSD specific info. He plans to send me docs regarding PSD specific projects they did. He did comment that value chain is a high level esoteric concept that doesn't translate well to Afghans- and stated they did limited PSD and treated it like a second order effect.]

Lessons Learned Record of Interview

Project Title	
LLP01 – Strategy and Planning	
Interview Code:	
LL-01 (b)(3), (b)(6)	
Date/Time:	
August 25, 2015 / 14:30 – 15:30	
Location:	
Washington, DC	
SIGAR Attendees:	
Candace Rondeaux, Matthew Sternenberger	

Non- attribution Basis:	Yes	x	No	
Recorded:	Yes		No	x

Recording File Record Number:
Prepared By: (Name, title and date)
Matthew Sternenberger, Research Analyst, 8/26/2015
Reviewed By: (Name, title and date)
Key Topics:
<ul><li>Afghanistan overview</li><li>Observations and Examples with Oversight Mechanisms</li><li>Necessary Introspection</li><li>PRTs and Logistics</li><li>Current Critiques of Strategy and SIGAR</li><li>International Perspective</li><li>Lessons</li></ul>

Afghanistan Overview

(b)(3), (b)(6), (b)(7)(C), (b)(7)(D)

Most Americans hold the view that the strategy in Afghanistan has not succeeded and the rest believe that there are many other places much more dangerous than Afghanistan; it is an uphill battle to the U.S. Overall, it seems that security assistance is less vulnerable and slower to temper – likely because it is structured differently and now under Overseas Contingency Operations.

Observations and Examples with Oversight Mechanisms

What surprises me is that you are talking to National Security Council (NSC) people and not with people from the U.S. Agency for International Development (USAID). The NSC is supposed to track implementation ensure that resources are going toward the intended objectives. While we are tasked to track this

Lessons Learned Record of Interview

implementation, we must get our information from the relevant agencies. There is no independent stream of information and our job is to hold them accountable. It is obvious that there is a disconnect between the strength of our core investments and our desired affects. We must give people a discount that has not been afforded to them. For example, we question USAID on a program they are implementing, but should we even be doing that program in the first place? There is a bigger question here – why does the U.S. undertake actions that are beyond its abilities? This question gets at strategy and human psychology, and it is a hard question to answer. It [Afghanistan] is not government-in-a-box or nation-building. The military is equally as guilty too of biting off more than they can chew. Development is more criticized, in part, due to the SIGAR mandate but the Department of Defense (DOD) Operations and Maintenance (O&M) costs are not under equal scrutiny. USAID is over-scrutinized.

USAID and the DOD have different barriers to scrutiny. While it is true there is a lot of scrutiny, it is grossly insufficient regarding the DOD O&M and conflict. We just don't question the DOD in the same way as we question development agencies in conflict zones. **"We don't scrutinize DOD fuel costs because we have institutionalized it and adopted a "that's how it goes" notion."** We have formalized $100 per gallon as normal for the DOD. This is potentially a bad way of warfighting.

There have been some people in the Pentagon who are looking at this, but they have been doing it is private or semi-private. If we look at the Mine-Resistant Ambush Protected (MRAP) program [vehicle]. We had a surge of MRAPs into Afghanistan to protect against $300 improvised explosive devices (IEDs). Now we have cut those [MRAPs] into razor blades. Is this just the cost of doing business? The full burden of the MRAP program seems to be just how we do business and not in support of the military or even in support of COIN.

When we look at COIN as economic assistance (digging wells or building school) and not as military tool, it looks like our spending was wasteful and ugly. One of [General] McChrystal's hardest lessons was his government-in-a-box program which typified the American wartime machinery and he thought you could simply wave a magic wand and POOF!

Necessary Introspection

Why did it get to this point? The answer is much broader than SIGAR and is about human psychology and national security policy making – the complexities will take a long time to unravel. Our entire post-9/11 response is all subject to question because of this increasing complexity. Why did we make the Taliban the enemy when we were attacked by Al Qaeda? Why did we want to defeat the Taliban? Why did we think it was necessary to build a hyper-function state to forgo the return of the Taliban? In fairness the people I know in government believed we were guilt of nation-building.

If the civilians are not doing their part, on rule of law or governance for example, is all this for not? Should we even do it? If this [rule of law and governance] is what the military needs, then the military may be forced to do it or contract it out.

"Ashraf Ghani was the original SIGAR." Ghani [then Minister of Finance] said, early on, that the methodology the U.S. had for building roads in Afghanistan was flawed and will have unintended consequences. USAID and State, said that we can't do it Ghani's way because we are not structurally equipped to do so. Ghani said that the U.S. should just give the money to the Afghans and they will build the roads and will likely do it at 1/10th of the cost but that is just not how we do economic assistance. We are not comfortable just writing a check and saying, go forth, do it.

Provincial Reconstruction Teams (PRT) and Logistics

PRTs would have been on Ghani's hit list. **"Administering aid through PRTs made sense on one level to synchronize efforts between the embassy and ISAF. It sounds good and works on PowerPoint."** It was really about coordination of strategy, a whole of government approach and wanting control.

Lessons Learned Record of Interview

"We have institutionalized the dysfunction because we want control of a synchronized strategy."

The MRAP is a prime example of this and so is the fuel distribution process – we transport fuel with helicopters to the provinces! Soldiers get pizza and ice cream while out in the provinces instead of getting food from local vendors. This is all happening because that is just the nature of the military logistical system.

Current Critiques of Strategy and SIGAR

Isaiah Wilson has written on the point that COIN has failed in the modern era. COIN forces today are disconnected from their area of operation and resupply is thousands of miles away. Instead of seeking security from the community, they hide in MRAPs; instead of sourcing food locally, they have it imported. ***"The modern COIN forces are like aliens parachuting in and staying only for short rotations with no sense of the landscape."***

Economic development efforts have not been just wasteful but have been institutionalized within COIN in unique ways which need to be re-examined. Really, both the military and the civilian side need to have their structures re-examined. [Ambassador] Eikenberry also wrote a good critique, despite it being a bit personal, which hit many of these same themes.

It is understandable that it has been hard get at the ineffective or dysfunctional narrative. The hard question is how does this dysfunction happen? Most will eventually conclude that we should not have implemented the strategy that we did. There is a lot of noise over this disagreement because of SIGAR and how what SIGAR says is often seen as cheap shots at agencies just wasting money. But in the conflict zone and in the bureaucracy that is within, there is a larger infection and structural dysfunction. People are quite defensive because there often is no context [to SIGAR's reports] and the reports are seen in an accusatory way.

People have said and continue to say that Afghanistan has improved despite all of these mistakes. When authors are making this claim they run through a long list of metrics about mortality, education, nutrition etc.

I would argue that it is all similarly and structurally handicapped. Like how COIN is grossly ineffective because of the complicated environments. That said, it is less a target since the inefficiencies in the DOD O&M far exceed civilian agencies waste during peak war. For example, there is $120 billion for DOD O&M, $12 billion for security assistance and $2.5 billion for civil development. The focus seems to be on the $12 billion or the $2.5 billion and never on the $120 billion for the DOD. The DOD is not just a job program for the U.S. Army and the affects may be more adverse than most know (care for wounded, costs of PTSD etc), but this critique is missing.

Overall it was our assumption that security would improve from 2008 to 2012 as we increased resources and that we would see a return on our investment. Generals Petraeus and Allen had faith that what happened in Iraq would happen in Afghanistan, but that never materialized. In terms of the big picture, there were many questions that were not uncovered because there was no reason to look at certain issues and also SIGAR came into being. ***"We were just moving too fast, with too many people and too many resources."*** The big picture question is also about what are we doing here [in Afghanistan]? What did we get for this $1 trillion effort? Was it worth $1 trillion? These conversations are only happening in private.

After the killing of Osama Bin Laden, I said that Osama was probably laughing in his watery grave considering how much we have spent on Afghanistan. Tom Donnelly always was asking for cost comparisons to other programs [both domestic and international].

Collectively the system is incapable of taking a step back to question basic assumptions. Again, I point to human psychology as to why this is difficult. [This resistance to introspection] is hard wired in us and part of our evolution.

Lessons Learned Record of Interview

International Perspective

Most people, even in Europe offer criticism and those we should take seriously but still they believe that some response [to the attacks on 9/11] was warranted. They also say that the U.S. response exceeded what was necessary. This includes the over-aggregation of the enemy to include the Taliban as part of our response to al Qaeda. Why, if we were focused on al Qaeda, were we talking about the Taliban? Why were we talking about the Taliban all the time instead of focusing our strategy on al Qaeda?

Micah Zenko recently wrote about the myth of terrorist safe havens and this question about why al Qaeda was connected to the Taliban through this safe haven defense. **Chris Fair** also just published an article about how Pakistan is really the big problem and that it is time we take the kids gloves off.

We have tied ourselves in a Gordian knot. The knot is that while the C. Fair article makes sense, it was not true for most of the period as we did have an al Qaeda-focused strategy and we had to get in bed with and acknowledge that Pakistan was a state sponsor of terrorism, but the Taliban was not as high on the list of priorities for us. We had to work with Pakistan to get to al Qaeda despite Pakistan helping the Taliban. Al Qaeda was a higher strategic objective. Maybe C. Fair's argument is better received now, but that was not always true; we can't sacrifice our top priority.

Lessons

1. Choose your enemies wisely. I recently wrote a piece on this for Foreign Policy (they changed the title however).
2. Don't over-aggregate the enemy.
3. Militarizing a response to criminal attack will lead to a host of problems (terrorism is a criminal act, not an act of war).
4. The process for monitoring and implementing strategy lacks introspection. There is too much momentum and not enough reflection.
5. Staying the course is a costly fallacy.
6. National pride and politics matter as they did in the 2003 invasion and the 2008 [U.S.] elections – both contributed to the problem. Obama simplified the narrative into a good war (Afghanistan) versus bad war (Iraq) theme. It was a useful narrative for the 2008 elections and then it all fell apart and became a liability.

LESSONS LEARNED RECORD OF INTERVIEW

Project Title and Code:	
LL-01 – Strategy and Planning	
Interview Title:	
Interview Ambassador Richard Boucher, former Assistant Secretary of State for South and Central Asian Affairs.	
Interview Code:	
LL-01-b9	
Date/Time:	
10/15/2015; 15:10-16:45	
Location:	
Providence, RI	
Purpose:	
To elicit his officials from his time serving as Assistant Secretary of State for South and Central Asian Affairs.	
Interviewees: (Either list interviewees below, attach sign-in sheet to this document or hyperlink to a file)	
SIGAR Attendees:	
Matthew Sternenberger, Candace Rondeaux	
Sourcing Conditions (On the Record/On Background/etc.):	On the record.
Recorded: Yes	x	No	
Recording File Record Number (if recorded):	
Prepared By: (Name, title and date)	
Matthew Sternenberger	
Reviewed By: (Name, title and date)	
Key Topics:	

- General Observations
- The State and DOD Struggle
- Building Security Forces
- Governance Expectations and Karzai
- Capable Actors
- Regional Economics and Cooperation
- General Comments on Syria & Iraq
- Lessons Learned

General Observations

Let me approach this from two directions. The first question of did we know what we were doing? The second is what was wrong with how we did it? The first question of did we know what we were doing – I think the answer is no. First, we went in to get al-Qaeda, and to get al-Qaeda out of Afghanistan, and even without killing Bin Laden we did that. The Taliban was shooting back at us so we started shooting at them and they became the enemy. Ultimately, we kept expanding the mission. George W. [Bush], when he was running for president, said that the military should not be involved in nation building. In the end, I think he was right. **If there was ever a notion of mission creep it is Afghanistan.** We went from saying we will get rid of al-Qaeda so they can't threaten us

LESSONS LEARNED RECORD OF INTERVIEW

anymore to saying we are going to end the Taliban. [Then we said] that we will get all of the groups the Taliban works with. [Then further to having] our exit strategy be a stable government in Afghanistan. Once you start saying that and you start getting into stable government, democratic elections, making sure the Supreme Court functions properly, anti-corruption authority, and a women's ministry that looks at women's rights, new educational curriculum, transitional justice (which means you will go after all the people the president relies upon for political support). You are trying to build systematic government à la Washington, DC, which is not the best example but that is the one we have in our hands, in a country that doesn't operate that way. If we think our exit strategy is to either beat the Taliban, which can't be done given the local, regional, and cross-border circumstances, or to establish an Afghan government that is capable of delivering good government to its citizens using American tools and methods, then we have no exit strategy because both of those are impossible. If we defined our exit strategy as leaving a more or less functional Afghanistan, that wouldn't be a harbor for al-Qaeda, maybe we could have got at that properly. Train up an army, let Karzai have money to distribut (b)(1) - 1.4(D)

We did not know what we were doing. First, maybe everybody may should have had to read a little more history besides just Ghost Wars to operate in Afghanistan. The only time this country [Afghanistan] has worked properly was when it was a floating pool of tribes and warlords presided over by someone who had a certain eminence who was able to centralize them to the extent that they didn't fight each other too much. I think this idea that we went in with that this was going to become a state government like a U.S. state or something like that was just wrong and is what condemned us to 15 years of war instead of 2 or 3.

The other big problem is me, you and Jessie Helms. Jessie Helms because when the Soviet Union fell apart, we had to cut a deal with Jessie Helms to continue our aid programs. The deal with Jessie Helms was that we would spend the money in the United States. We would buy American products, American grain, American consultants, American Security experts, and they would implement our aid programs. Those billions of dollars you guys were trying to track down, I mean you must be able to find this number. The Afghans used to tell me that somewhere between 10-20% actually shows up in Afghanistan, and less than 10% ever gets to a village. So you tell us [the Afghans] that you just spent a billion dollars as we see $50 million worth of roads. You [the U.S.] hire a big contractor and inside the beltway consultant, who then hires 15 subcontractors. The first guy takes 20%, then next level takes 20% who would go hire a bunch of expensive American experts to do what Afghan diaspora refugees or Indian experts could do for ten times the price. [These Americans we hire] travel to Afghanistan first class or at least business class with five security guys each. Then you come and maybe you do training for the same group of people that have been trained 12 times by different countries or you go out to the village to build a school and that is very nice. The money you spend doesn't get to the village, doesn't really help the Afghan government.

We were sort of aware of this. We took the Afghans seriously on this. Bill Wood and I pushed to push more money through the Afghan government gradually. This is 7 or 8 years after we first arrived in Afghanistan. We started putting some money through certain ministries that had been able to qualify for the accountability of U.S. assistance. I am afraid that is the second problem – the fact that there is an institution that is trying to account for every dollar we spend in Afghanistan. You can't do that. You can't spend money and track money at the same time in Afghanistan. Larry Summers used to talk about dropping money from a helicopter in order to stimulate the economy, sometimes you have to do that. Sometimes you just have to spend money and hope that it is useful or assume that some of it will disappear – that a large chunk will disappear in Afghanistan. You can do somethings to account for it better like get receipts and ask the governors and ministers you give it to, to submit an accounting of how they spend it. If you think you can go and audit every gun, box of nails, and bag of cement, you are just fooling yourself. Congress unfortunately thinks that we can.

LESSONS LEARNED RECORD OF INTERVIEW

That is where part of the problem is me. **People like me that didn't go up to Congress and say "40% of this money will disappear – I guarantee it.** I will do my best to make sure we know where it goes. I will make sure it is spent as usefully as possible given the circumstance. But 40% is going to disappear and I just want you to know that upfront. I want it to disappear in Afghanistan, rather than in the beltway. So, give me less money and let me spend it in Afghanistan through the government and then ask the government what they do with it." **Not only that, but probably in the end it is going to make sure that more of the money gets to some villager, maybe through five layers of corrupt officials, but still gets to some villager. It also will build a capability, an allegiance, and a dependency on the government.** Because we don't trust the [Afghan] government we go out and spend the money through American contractors, American NGOs, and the American military.

The CERP program the military has is a great program. They go out there, sit down with villagers and talk about what they need – schools? Roads? Trainings? How can we help you get competitive bidding, local contractors? You would talk to the majors and they have all these great programs that will now leave when the major leaves, or when the U.S. military leaves. That doesn't build any Afghan government capability. That actually undercuts the government. (b)(1) - 1.4(B), 1.4(D) Yeah, the major would bring a local official along for the ride, but everybody knew who had the checkbook.

We shouldn't fool ourselves about where the money goes, it is more important about how we spend the money. The political affect with having the [Afghan] government deliver something to the people, even if it is the chance to pull 20% more off their cut in Afghanistan. It means we are establishing the government as the course of benefits. We ought to work hard to make sure the government distributes the benefits fairly, but we ought to not try to distribute that stuff ourselves which is essentially what we did...because of me, you and Jessie Helms.

So we ran a parallel system of aid and development in Afghanistan and then we left. Now that we are going to have fewer troops even at the levels the president is announcing today, Army contractors aren't going to be out there. Maybe, we will have to deliver assistance through the Afghan government. There are a few Afghan programs that were good, the solidarity program was good. We tried to make sure they kept getting money from us, but never as much as others. Health ministry was doing pretty well. **As far as I know, we didn't build roads through the Ministry of Public Works. We didn't just turn over money to the Ministry of Education to run the schools. I think, in the end, we did them a disservice by not doing that.**

Now there is another problem and it goes back the structure of government. We want a government to be setup according to an org chart with all kinds of democratic elections. Jelani Popal, had an office of local governance in Karzai's office. We tried, with him, to set up a fund. Trying to get him $50 million that he could use to put money into districts that he trusted, that they trusted, that the palace thought was responsive to them. His relations with Karzai did not work out. **I think that because in the end, Karzai's governing instincts** (b)(1) - 1.4(D) **were to rely on his friends. That is how Afghanistan works – relying on his friends, supporters, and local potentates; powers that be, not just powers that the American's created.** (b)(1) - 1.4(B), 1.4(D) So getting him to use that governing structure that we put in place, that we told him he had to have, was really hard. So getting money into the provinces and districts, and having the central government and Karzai use that chain, was hard. He relied on his friends in provinces for information for what was really going on. He relied on them for his political support and favors. They relied on him for the same. We didn't accept that that was the way things work in Afghanistan. We said, you have to work through this democratic, bureaucratic system just like what have in America. We were consistently a quarter turn off from Karzai that eventually produced some blow ups and dust ups that we had with him.

The State and DOD Struggle

LESSONS LEARNED RECORD OF INTERVIEW

Iran is very interesting. Rahmon in Tajikistan, when we built them a bridge, then said to me soon after, "okay you have to build me a train to go across the bridge." I asked why? He said that "if I get a train across the bridge then you need to build a train across the north to Iraq and on into Iran. That way I can export through Iranian ports." I said, "I am sorry, the U.S. government is not in the business of creating new trade with Iran. We have sanctions and embargoes and not in the position to do that." But if you are sitting in Central Asia, we have blinders on. We say, "Look! Great gas lines through war-torn Iraq, through messed dup Pakistan, and may even through India where they will cooperate. They would probably make you offload the gas on the Indian side just like they do the trucks.

So I think, in the end, it made sense in a strategic way, but in a political and practical way, no. This is what I am trying to teach my kids in class – that is may make sense in policy terms but you still have to deal with personalities in politics.

General Comments on Syria & Iraq

There is a whole other set of lessons from Iraq that would apply more to Syria than Afghanistan does. That is de-Ba'athification. You can chop the head off the Mr. Potato Head but then the arms and legs continued to run the country. Afghanistan didn't have that core, they had some, but not like Iraq or Syria where they had people who could make the electricity go and water run.

5 months ago I wrote a blog post about the Sandinista solution for Syria. In the end Reagan could not defeat the Sandinistas with an insurgency so under pressure from Congress and the Central Americans, he negotiated and got them to agree to an election. Against most people's bets, they [the Sandinistas] lost the elections. Get the other side to agree to a U.N. supervised election in two years and say that we will cooperate with you. Just have to trust the people of Syria to make the right choice.

LESSONS LEARNED RECORD OF INTERVIEW

(b)(1) - 1.4(D)

(b)(1) - 1.4(B), 1.4(D)

(b)(1) - 1.4(B), 1.4(D)

I think the answer is yes, [that we can partner with a nation like Pakistan]. Many of us have thought the answer was yes and many of us were willing to spend money there even though a bunch of it would be wasted. I think the answer is yes for two reasons. First, fundamentally our interests are similar. Stability, trade, modernization.

(b)(1) - 1.4(B), 1.4(D)

LESSONS LEARNED RECORD OF INTERVIEW

no money, no currency, no foreign reserves, no gold and none of what you would expect. Most of the ministries didn't have a telephone, I forget how many fax machines. Somehow the Afghans managed to put on this amazing lunch. This huge banquet with piles of rice and dead goats. **They were capable people but they didn't want anything to run a government with so it really was from scratch both organizationally and materially. I think we never let them take the lead and maybe that is just a result of the fact that we found Karzai and flown him in and told everybody that he was their leader. We never even waited for the Afghans to organize themselves.** If it had been a table of Karzai and Ismail Khan, he might have been there since he was energy minister for a while and Dostum Even Hekmatyar and other nasty warlord guys form different tribes and half of Karzai's Pashtun friends from the south, we would have found it distasteful, but it might have worked out better.

When I first got the job in 2006, on one of my first trips out to Kabul, the DEA Administrator was there. He was going up to Jalalabad, so I went with him to Jalalabad and Sherzai was governor. (b)(1) - 1.4(D) I asked him what he needs in terms of construction here. He said, "I need 5 schools, 5 colleges, 5 dams, and 5 highways." I said well how come? He said "well I need to the highways so the farmers can deliver their food, the schools so kids gets educated here and don't go to Pakistan madrassas, dams for irrigation and electricity." I said, well okay, but why 5? He said "I got this tribe, this tribe, this tribe, this tribe, and one for everybody else." I thought that was the funniest thing I ever heard and now I think it is now one of the smartest thing I ever heard but we weren't prepared to work through that system. We weren't prepared to build up governors and people who weren't behold to the central government and people who would probably take 20% for personal use or for their extended families and friends.

It was more and more frustrating [for Karzai], and I don't know if you talked with Bill Wood or the CIA folks or some general who knew him. (b)(1) - 1.4(B), 1.4(D)

We didn't intentionally go and say, here is bullet, please shoot an American, but the fact that some of our stuff go to the Taliban through fairly direct means was probably true. I probably should have taken him more seriously.

(b)(1) - 1.4(D)

hate corruption and have worked anti-corruption all over the world but there are different kinds of corruption. There is corruption that spreads the wealth and takes care of everybody, gets to the orphans and widows. Then there is corruption that goes to my house on the Riviera. I think Afghanistan has a lot more of the orphans and widows, with a few warlords in between, and a lot less of the house on the Riviera type of corruption.

Capable Actors

LESSONS LEARNED RECORD OF INTERVIEW

The other thing is that there were all type of capable Afghans in the diaspora and rather than bringing in people from Washington or Rumsfeld cronies, why didn't we do a better job recruiting from the Afghan diaspora? Probably because they didn't want to go back. The ministers I worked with were [from the diaspora]. Spanta was a German university professor and Rassoul was a doctor. Also, why weren't we hiring Pakistanis and Indians? Each one of them has a political problem associated within, but still as U.S. government contractors, they could have done stuff in certain sectors. I think that if we could have figured a way to get the Indian Election Commission in there to run elections instead of Americans that would have been good. (b)(1) - 1.4(B), 1.4(D)

Regional Economics and Cooperation

It [a focus on the regional aspects] was in Bonn. It should have been in Bonn. That was the moment that you could go to all the regional players and ask what type of Afghanistan do we want? What kind of government do we want in Afghanistan? How do we support it? I didn't do that. **I had people like (b)(1) - 1.4(D) telling me that there needs to be a regional conference to decide the future of Afghanistan. I would say no. There is a government in Afghanistan and they will have to decide the future of Afghanistan and we can help you have a good relationship with them.** We can help do other regional things like electricity lines, exchanges and all that stuff. We can't have people from the outside deciding the fate of Afghanistan – they have to do that themselves. I was pretty strong on that. **I know Holbrooke, when he came in, he started organizing regional meetings and having everyone appointed as special envoy for Afghanistan and having big meetings. I hope he enjoyed it but, you're not going to fix Afghanistan from the outside in, you're going to fix it from the ground up inside Afghanistan.**

I used to talk about ground-up security. If you could start to establish decent government and include locals, you can build the nation from there. That is why police were so important to me. That is why roads were so important to me. I am not sure it worked, but it at least occasionally showed some promise. I had a different model for elections – maybe starting with local and district level elections. Sort of an Indian rotational system. Just the way the U.S. started – having the districts elect the districts elect the provincial leaders and have the provincial leaders getting together to elect the central leader; do an adaption of Karzai's tribal coalition approach. That is the way the [U.S.] Senate is not directly elected and the president is still not directly elected. Something like that, which builds the nation from the ground up and provide a place for everybody. Yes, in some places, the village leader will say everyone has to vote for my son, that's fine. His son and everybody else's son will get together and select provincial leaders and so on. That kind of system is more adapted to a place with that local thing. I resisted the idea of fixing Afghanistan from the outside.

I tried to get neighbors to cooperate and support. It was much easier with Central Asia as Afghanistan was their route to the sea. Even with **Turkmenistan,** (b)(1) - 1.4(D)

We had a big energy conference that is when Ismail Khan was in Istanbul. We actually had some Columbians come and brief how they maintain gas pipelines during an insurgency. It turns out it is not that hard to do. You just have be able to fix things quickly. They can blow it up at any point, but you have to be able to get out there and fix it pretty quick as people are relying on the gas supply. Also you get locals to buy in to the work and repairs and sometimes the gas. Then we talked a lot about powerlines coming down from Kazahkstan, Kyrgystan, and Tajikistan. Bob Deutch, who is now living in Florida, was my guy who would do regional stuff in that regard. So the idea was to knit the region together with gas, electricity and trade.

LESSONS LEARNED RECORD OF INTERVIEW

There were these periodic economic meetings – first one of which I went to was in Kabul. Then we had one in India in about 2008 or 2007. The **Indians**, being very protocol conscious, didn't care I was the American, I was only an Assistant Secretary. So after all the others spoke who were allotted ten minutes each, I got three minutes. My speech was about fruit. I basically said there are Indian and Pakistani oranges in the markets in Osh, we need to make sure melons from Osh can make it to the breakfast tables in New Delhi. The fact is that they couldn't. They couldn't because of corruption. They couldn't because of borders, the Indian-Pakistan dispute, and trucking. You had to offload and then on load at the India-Pakistan border and all types of other rules. But the best melons in the world are from the Fergana Valley and yet they had no way of getting to the breakfast tables of New Delhi. We tried to work on it, but I am afraid a lot of things that made it impossible like the India-Pakistan dispute, which I guess was off my vague radar although I tried. In the end, the Pakistanis didn't want us to solve their problems for the sake of melons from Fergana Valley. They would pay lip service to us then go back to their usual spats. Or because the border problems were not hard, but soft – bribes, corruptions, licenses delays. We build a bridge across the river Panj. I went with Secretary Gutierrez and Karzai. We flew up to Tajikistan and then flew down to the bridge by helicopter with President Rahmon to open the bridge. The band played and the dancers danced. I doubt if even more than two trucks a week go across that bridge, but it is a wonderful bridge. So we tried and kept trying. Eventually, it made sense political problems and corruption were very hard to overcome. **I guess, if we knew how to get over the political problems and the corruption problems, it wouldn't take a bridge to get the melons across…the melons would role from the Fergana Valley to the breakfast tables in New Delhi.**

In terms of regional security issues, we didn't too much with guys in the north. We did do counter drug operations. Russians turned out to be very good partners in that. I was just sort of the one pouring holy water on it and then the DEA guys were doing stuff with their **Russian** counterparts. Controlled delivers [for example] and some of the **Central Asians** were good on that too – to follow a package all the way across and figure out who was in the supply chain and how it was getting to Europe. We did that better and more than the Europeans. The French has a big counternarcotic conference at the Intercontinental [he believes] in Paris. Secretary Powell and made a speech. The French and others made speeches about how this is an awful problem and that we have to do something about it. We said, "excuse us, we have been doing something about it for seven years." These drugs are not coming to U.S., they are coming to Amsterdam. They are coming to Europe. We are actually surprised that you guys just discovered there is a problem. Then the French had their conference and said that they have to do something. Then they went back to their usual habits. The Russians and some of the Central Asians turned out to be pretty good. Afghan DEA guys turned out to be pretty good. Our DEA guys always wanted more money and more capability because they were just THAT close to catching the big fish. I have been fishing too and had my bait in the water a long time and never caught the big fish.

Eradication was complicated. (b)(1) - 1.4(B), 1.4(D)

Then you had the Washington Post stories and U.S. troops walking through fields of poppy while on patrol and not doing anything about it. I sympathize with the troops if I was in my flak jacket and there was poppy – I would just say they were pretty flowers. They were not there to start chopping flowers and then have someone start shooting at you.

The security part to the north – the **Uzbeks** often recognized the fact that we were working to get Uzbek militants and radicals in Afghanistan. We were sort of taking care of one of their problems. (b)(1) - 1.4(D)

We used to have regular consultations with the **Chinese** because there were some Uighurs in Afghanistan, the Taliban and al-Qaeda. (b)(1) - 1.4(D)

LESSONS LEARNED RECORD OF INTERVIEW

(b)(1) - 1.4(D)

People say you [Boucher] should write your memoirs. I would say I don't know what my book is about and if I could write the **Pakistan** chapter – the rest would be easy. I am still not as clear on Pakistan as I should be but I will get there someday. The best book I ever read on Pakistan was given to me by (b)(1) - 1.4(D) He gave me the book called "Report on Waziristan and its Tribes." It is a collection of British dispatches from the late 19th century and how they tried to subdue Pashtuns. It goes through a series of steps they took. One was that they tried to beat the military which they could do. Two, they tried to turn the tribes against themselves – that didn't work. Three, they tried to invite the leaders and chiefs for education, basically hold them hostage. The tribal leaders were smart enough to know what was going on so they sent the sons of their slaves or their underlings so that didn't work very well. It goes through a whole series of measures. What they finally did was put the tribal chiefs on their payroll and when the tribe was acting up or someone in the tribe committed a murder was to be turned over, they cut off the paycheck. I presume the guy's wife would start complaining and his underlings would start complaining that they weren't getting their money that month and they would come to the Brits and cut a deal. Then they would start the payroll again.

That was what the Pakistanis took over – that system of tribal allegiance and payoffs. Pakistan treated the tribal areas separate and still had that system nominally in place into 2006 and 2007. They finally passed some laws to change it but not enough. That was the nominal system, but what happened was that during the 1980s we destroyed that system by funneling money and guns through the mullahs and the military and the militant groups. We created, in the tribal areas, a mullah-military-militant complex to fight the Soviets. They were very good at it. They got a lot of money. They got a lot of weapons. We destroyed the social fabric and governing structure. Both the Pakistani governing structure of tribal agents and the tribal governing structures. It was no longer the chief, the elders, the people who had been around, or the paterfamilias. The paterfamilias' of the families were no longer really the guys in charge. The people with money and capability were the preacher that had a madrassa, the military commander, and the head of the militant group. Those were the people, like Haqqani, who had the right name, but essentially he was able to govern because he had that authority from the war against the Soviets. **So we basically setup an ungoverned space. A very militant ungoverned space. That is what we had to deal with when we got back to Afghanistan.**

Countless times we had consultations across the border, we occasionally had coordination across the border where we would say to the Pakistan military that we need to move in this direction (Nuristan was one place) and as we moved into Nuristan, they did some stuff on the other side of the border that was pretty effective. That type of coordination worked for a while until some of our guys would shoot at the Pakistan border post, or the Special Forces got so envious of drone strikes that they had to say we can also do that on the ground too and come back with cell phones and information. So we let them go across the border once and that was a fiasco. I don't think it was unclassified, but it was reported in the media so I am basing this off press releases. Again, we thought the Pakistani military would take care of its problem for us. We went to countless meetings where the Pakistanis would stand up, since they were all educated at U.S. war colleges, and tell us about the reform of the Pakistani Army and that they were putting more people into counterinsurgency training and devoting less forces to the

LESSONS LEARNED RECORD OF INTERVIEW

sectorial problems. This is a problem we have had all over the world and haven't solved very well. Like in Bosnia. You take the lid of the secular dictator off. You get rid of Tito, and you get sectarian violence. You get rid of Saddam and you get sectarian violence in Iraq. You get rid of Kaddafi, you get sectarian violence in Libya. You get rid of Assad and you bet you will have the same thing.

In some ways sectarian dictatorships are pretty good. The Turkish model is hard to implement in some of these places, because they don't like the Turks and don't want to be seen as Turks. They didn't like the Ottoman Empire. We don't really have a strategy for dealing with this and again the problem is the military's can-do attitude. Everything in Washington is either a testosterone test or a job for Special Forces. It is about time someone said hold it! It should be about 1/3 military, 1/3 regional players, and 1/3 governance on the ground. There is 2/3rds we are not doing right now. Foreign policy is fun until you have to go somewhere with bullets flying in the air and you have to fix it.

Lessons Learned

1. Lower your expectations.
2. Define your goals.
3. Don't forget why you went there.
4. Mission creep is inherent in our system.
5. We have to say good enough is good enough. That is why we are there 15 years later. We are trying to achieve the unachievable instead of achieving the achievable.
6. If governance is your exit strategy, as it almost always is when we go into these places, we have to get a lot better at building governance. Not great, not systematic, not accountable, just decent governance.

LESSONS LEARNED RECORD OF INTERVIEW

There was another part of that we, State Department, did wrong. **We started out in Afghanistan with this attitude that we will do the military, the Germans, will do the police, and the Italians will do the justice system. Everybody was going to take a sector. Then of course, nobody had the resources. Nobody had the capabilities. Nobody had the determination in the other sectors or at least not to our liking.** The Germans were training police hierarchy officers, but not placemen, thinking that somehow good officers would filter down. They didn't understand that the central officers had very little control over the behavior of local policemen. That was true place after place. If you look at it after 15 years, we could have taken a thousand school children in first grade, well not quite first but fifth grade, and taken them to get educated and trained in Indian schools and colleges. Then we could have brought them back on an airplane by now and said ok you guys run Afghanistan. I am not sure that would have worked any better. Better than having a bunch of Americans going in and saying we can build it for you, with you, meaning you can come to my meetings and listen to me go on and on. I think part of it was Defense wanting to skedaddle, and this idea that you can have different sectors run by different countries. **Part of it was that we trained people to be Americans, the Germans trained people to be Germans, and the Italians trained people to be Italians.** Some of the Afghans remained Afghans.

Governance Expectations and Karzai

One of the things I am going to give a speech on soon is [expectations of governance]. One of our global problems is that now people care about the quality of governance and the fairness of governance. The fact that you have explosions in Ukraine, Syria, Iraq and elsewhere, is because they are not getting fair and decent government. You had the Arab Spring because the middle class was demanding fairness from their government. When you look around the world and where have we done a good job helping people develop better governments, government institutions and fair systematic governance for their people? There is a lot of stuff now in the development scheme and that is why countries develop and that's why they prosper. It is not money or investment, but it is a stable government institution. So where have we done that well? We have done it pretty well helping out in Taiwan, Korea and Singapore, but they were all dictatorships or autocracies for a long time and that is not exactly a model we want to propose you use elsewhere. We did it pretty well in Eastern Europe when they got out of the Soviet Bloc but they just woke up in the morning and said "I want to do that" and pointed at Europe. They said "how do Europeans brush their teeth? That is how I am going to brush my teeth." They said "how do they control their currencies? That is how I am going to control my currency." They all this body of EU law that they could go and apply. The ones that did it more thoroughly are doing better now but that was fairly straightforward for them.

The only other places we have done a good job bringing good governance is where they decided that they were going to finally try to reform and do it right. Chile unfortunately a dictatorship model and we most contributed by training their people in Chicago. Columbia, Plan Columbia worked because it was a Columbian plan that we helped with once the Columbians decided they were going to take their problems on a fix them. Georgia is starting to look that way now. Philippines will look that way. But who knows how much money we have thrown into the Philippines over the years. Yes, the rice thing in the 1960s was great, but in terms of stable prosperity governance, they are getting their act together now and we want to help. So we don't really have that many good models and we certainly don't have many good models for countries as destitute as Afghanistan was.

When we first went there with Secretary Powell, Ryan Crocker and the Embassy were already there. They were living in something called the bunker. It had been built in the Najib period or early Soviet period. It had two wings – the boys wing and the girls wing. That is where they slept. They had a little place to cook. They worked in the embassy, but it was missing certain amenities like plumbing so they couldn't really live there. Actually the day the Powell visited, they got the toilets to work. In terms of the lives of the people on the compound, that was probably a bigger deal than the Secretary of State coming to visit. We went to a cabinet meeting with Karzai and he had 30 people around the table. He had his Minister for Women's Affairs, just like we told him he had to. He had all the ministers for justice and it was just like the American cabinet. They were sitting around but they had nothing. The central bank governor was telling us how he went and opened the vaults and there was nothing inside. There was

LESSONS LEARNED RECORD OF INTERVIEW

There are two reasons that [Congress is obsessed with the war fighting aspect of the intervention]. First, boys with toys. The Pentagon has all this cool stuff. I used to argue with my counterpart at Defense, Pete Williams when he was spokesman there and I was spokesman at State. [I would say to him that] you [Pete Williams] go up in your briefing and somebody asks about the Battleship Iowa lobbing shells into Lebanon. You tell where it was made, the names of the workers, the locations of the workers, and the congressional districts of everybody that made the shell, the gun, the metal. [You also tell them] where the commander was from, how many rounds, and how many that...all the boys with toys stuff. Then someone raises their hand asks why they are throwing shells into the side of Lebanon and he would refer them to the State Department, and that is my question. Congress is a bit like that too. They are fascinated by all this stuff that is built in their districts and they love the mechanical stuff.

The other problem, which is a problem Americans have, but especially the American military is the can-do attitude. It gets us into trouble. We think we are Mr. Fixit. The president goes around the table and says, "we have problem here." The first guy to raise his hand is the Special Forces guy who says they can take care of it. [The president might also ask why] our aid is not getting down to the district level – the military steps up and says, sir we have $100 million in CERP programs and we can increase that to $200 million. We have majors, people all over the country that can take care of that for you. That is the wrong way to do it. **It is better to do it badly through an Afghan civilian government structure perhaps with some civilian advisors, than to do it ourselves well, through the military.** Something everybody in Afghanistan knows, except the U.S. military is that eventually the U.S. military leaves and all of these capabilities, all these toys, all these programs, leave with them. I am not surprised, but it takes a bit of a mindset change.

One thing I complain about all the time now is the sort of militarization of foreign policy. That is where the money is, the military has the money and the can-do attitude. Ask the State Department guy to do it and he says, "that is really complicated." It doesn't sound like the right answer when you are trying to get something done, but it is unfortunately frequently the truth...it is really complicated. You can just go play whack-a-mole with the Taliban or drop drones on people and think you are solving the problem. [You can't also] just throw more military advisors into an army that is not capable of doing anything like in Iraq. "I can take care of that for you Mr. President" is probably the worst answer, but it is often the one that gets the applause and it usually gets applause on the hill too.

Building Security Forces

The thinking wasn't in Afghanistan, it was in State Department, it was Rumsfeld [on our decision to go light footprint]. It was that we should get rid of the government, then throw some money in there. **There were the Friends of Don [Rumsfeld].** He had one guy who knew electricity, one guy that knew water, one guy that knew health. They had a formal name and stationed in the embassy – the [Afghan] Reach Back Group. They were just on their way out when I was getting in around 2006. What did they know about Afghanistan? You know? **What were they doing in an Embassy with more money and responsibility, at least in the sector, than the Ambassador?** This was his way of saying, we got rid of al-Qaeda, you now reconstruct Afghanistan – I am going to Iraq. So the money and the troops went to Iraq. By the time I got there in 2006 to 2007, we hadn't hardly trained any Afghan police. There was no structure or capability to send police into localities and districts. So we ramped up that program. Got in a bureaucratic fight over who was going to run it and frankly I didn't care that much. So we started training policemen and setting up the kind of electronic payment system for their paychecks that we set up for the military four years before. General Cohen, at one point, was doing that training. He said, **"I know that we trained 70,000 policeman. I know we are paying 70,000 policeman. I just don't know if we are paying the 70,000 policemen we trained."** But that was Afghanistan, and you had to accept that type of situation if you were going to work there.

Printed in Great Britain
by Amazon